ACADEMIC INSTINCTS

MARJORIE GARBER

PRINCETON UNIVERSITY PRESS · PRINCETON AND OXFORD

Published by Princeton University Press, 41 William Street,
Princeton, New Jersey
In the United Kingdom: Princeton University Press,
3 Market Place, Woodstock, Oxfordshire OX20 1SY

Erich Lessing/Art Resource, NY
Reprinted with the permission of Simon & Schuster Books for
Young Readers, an imprint of Simon & Schuster Children's
Publishing Division, from *Alice in Wonderland* by Lewis Carroll,
illustrated by Sir John Tenniell (Macmillan, NY, 1963)
©The New Yorker Collection 2000 Roz Chast from cartoonbank.com.
All Rights Reserved.
Copyright, 1999, Danziger. Distributed by the
Los Angeles Times Syndicate. Reprinted with permission.

Library of Congress Cataloging-in-Publication Data
Garber, Marjorie B.
Academic Instincts / Marjorie Garber.
p.   cm.
Includes bibliographical references and index.
ISBN 0-691-04970-X
1. Humanities—Study and Teaching (Higher) 2. Literature—
Study and teaching (Higher) 3. Universities and colleges—Curricula.
4. Academic writing. 5. Humanities—Philosophy. 6. Learning
and scholarship. I. Title.
AZ182 .G37 2001
001.3'071'1—dc21   00-056510

This book has been composed in New Baskerville Typeface

The paper used in this publication meets the minimum requirements
of ANSI/NISO Z39.48-1992 (R1997) (*Permanence of Paper*)

www.pup.princeton.edu

Printed in the United States of America

1   3   5   7   9   10   8   6   4   2

For my graduate students,

past and present

CONTENTS

PREFACE

IN COMBINING the most "disciplined" and the most "undisciplined" of forces, the title *Academic Instincts* is meant to sound like a contradiction in terms. But this is a book about the energies that keep scholarly disciplines from becoming inert and settled. It is about the instincts not of individuals but of fields—what might be called the *disciplinary libido*. In each chapter, I consider the ways in which a field differentiates itself from, but also desires to become, its nearest neighbor, whether at the edges of the academy (the professional wants to be an amateur and vice versa), among the disciplines (each one covets its neighbor's insights), or within the disciplines (each one attempts to create a new language specific to its objects, but longs for a universal language understood by all). The chapters that follow thus address the current world of scholarship in the humanities in three different modes: through persons ("The Amateur Professional and the Professional Amateur"), institutions ("Discipline Envy"), and language ("Terms of Art").

I suggest that various attacks against the academic profession and various feuds within it—the disparagement of amateurs by professionals and professionals by amateurs, the desire to keep the disciplines pure, the accusation that academic writing is, unlike the language of the real world, jargon-ridden and incomprehensible—need to be reconceived. My fundamental argument has two strands. One is to show that these feuds are not stable. "Amateur," for example, functions as a term of praise during one period or if it comes from one direction, and as a term of abuse during another or if it springs from a different source. What is taken to contaminate different disciplines varies as the prestige (and intellectual accomplishments) of other disciplines change. Terms that are "jargon" today will be everyday language tomorrow. The other strand of my argument is to show that many of the contrasts around which these disputes revolve do not signify real opposites, but rather depend upon one another for their strength and effectiveness. In each case, I will maintain that the terms of praise or abuse have a double nature, and that it is important to acknowledge that doubleness. The doubleness, in other words, is in many ways more important than the positive or negative judgments the terms convey at any one time. The point is not to choose the right inflection for each term but to show how intellectual life arises out of their changing relationship to each other.

I should say something here about what this book is *not*. It is not a developmental history of the disciplines or of the profession of teaching English or the humanities. That work has been powerfully and effectively undertaken by scholars like Gerald Graff, John Guillory and W. Bliss Carnochan. This book is not the story of the encounter of the humanities with the world of science and social science, the world of "fact." That kind of work, too, has been well done, by Peter Galison and Mary Poovey among others. And this book is not the latest salvo in the so-called "culture wars," a formulation that was always more hype or buzz than pedagogical reality. I address these questions not to take a side in the polemic, nor to position myself above it, but to explore the ways in which these controversies are essential to the nature of intellectual life. The things deplored or defended in discussions of the humanities cannot be either eliminated or endorsed, because the discussion itself is what gives humanistic thought its vitality.

Scholars, despite what their critics say or what they themselves may claim, are basically conservative creatures (in the widest sense of that misused term), whose engagement with ideas and with students has been very much the same since the time of those renegade pedagogues, Plato and Aristotle. Despite the presence of Diogenes and of two delighted golden retrievers on the cover, there are no cynics in these pages, and relatively few, all things considered, in academic life. Teaching and writing at a college or university is a job for optimists and for idealists, whatever discursive or critical mode we may use in trying to shape ideas and the world.

So this book is not a history. It is an analysis, an intervention, and a credo. Although in the pages below I will make some pointed observations about the evocation of "love" in the teaching of the humanities, it would be fair to call this a love letter. A letter, sometimes critical, sometimes affectionate, always—I hope—passionate, addressed to a lifelong partner and companion, the profession of literary study.

ACADEMIC
INSTINCTS

1

THE AMATEUR PROFESSIONAL

AND

THE PROFESSIONAL AMATEUR

Criticism, is, I take it, the formal discourse
of an amateur. —R. P. BLACKMUR

THE ELECTION of Jesse ("The Body") Ventura, a former professional wrestler and radio talk-show host, as governor of Minnesota was described by the *New York Times* as an example of "the lure of inspired amateurism."[1] But of course American politicians have often tried to present themselves as amateurs, from George Washington to Ronald Reagan. Politics is a dirty business, and a professional politician an object of suspicion. Better to have a background in something, almost anything, else.

Like sports, for example. Former Senator Bill Bradley was a professional basketball player. Jack Kemp, a former housing secretary and candidate for vice president, was an NFL quarterback. Representative Steve Largent, the top draw for Republican fund-raisers in 1998, was a Hall of Fame wide receiver for the Seattle Seahawks. J. C. (Julius Caesar) Watts II was a college football star. "Let's hear it for the athlete as president!" said tennis player John McEnroe at a fund-raising rally in Madison Square Garden for candidate Bradley.[2]

Or consider, at least in the state of California, politicians from the world of entertainment. Not only Ronald Reagan but Sonny Bono, Clint Eastwood, George Murphy—and even, briefly, Warren Beatty. Or business. Think of the campaigns of Steve Forbes and Ross Perot, and even the trial balloon sent up by Donald Trump—all candidates who presented themselves as can-do men untainted by politics, bringing the power of their success in the marketplace to bear on national problems.

Disinterestedness seems to be an implied corollary of inexperience—or at least, inexperience *in the particular profession* to which the candidate aspired. Inexperience is just the experience the electorate often values most in its politicians. Amateur status, at least on the surface, seems to be a guarantor of virtue. Leave the rough stuff behind the scenes to the political operatives and the media consultants.

Still, it might be said, and quite properly, that politics is an unfair example. We don't so much value amateur surgeons, for example, or amateur lawyers. We live in a world of professionals and professionalization, from big league sports to massage therapy. Even something apparently impossible to professionalize, like "motivational speaking," is a high-paying job, performed by migrating professionals from other fields: Colin Powell, a retired army general and former chief of staff; Naomi Judd, a country-and-western singer; Terry Bradshaw, the former quarterback of the Pittsburgh Steelers; Mary Lou Retton, a gold-medal Olympic gymnast.

What I want to try to establish at the outset, though, is that, like the terms of any binary opposition, *amateur* and *professional* (1) are never fully equal, and (2) are always in each other's pockets. They produce each other and they define each other by mutual affinities and exclusions. One is always preferred to the other ("it's better to be an amateur"; "it's better to be a professional"), but the preference is not consistent over time. Indeed, what is most fascinating is the way in which these terms circulate to make the fortunes of the one rise higher than the fortunes of the other, while determinedly resisting the sense that one is always the necessary condition for the other.

Not only are they mutually interconnected. Part of their power comes from the disavowal of the close affinity between them.

Playing for Love

The apparent opposition of the terms "professional" and "amateur" is perhaps most familiar to us from the culture of sports, where until fairly recently "amateur" had a certain cachet and a certain association with the upper classes. The amateur was idealized as playing for "love"—love of the game, love of country, love of school. The professional, by contrast, played for advancement and for money.

In sport after sport, from football to boxing, the amateur/ professional distinction was once built in as part of the class structure of the sport. Amateurs were gentlemen; professionals were upstarts, class jumpers, and roughnecks. Aristocrats and gentry engaged in sporting events with the assistance of servants. Hunters had "gillies" or "beaters" to flush the game they shot, as well as gamekeepers to prevent poaching. Golfers were accompanied by "caddies," paid attendants who carried their clubs.

Here are a few examples of how this divide has been negotiated:

- Rugby associations at the end of the nineteenth century took steps to root out the "veiled professional," by which was meant the working-class player. "The Rugby name, as its name implies, sprang from our public schools," remarked one amateur rugby player and cricketer. "Why should we hand it over without a struggle to the hordes of working-men players who would quickly engulf all others?" Under pressure from amateurs, the sport split into two, with different rules and spirits: English Rugby Union, "the game of the public schools, the universities and the professions," and Rugby League, "deeply embedded in its northern working-class communities," and becoming "an important form of working-class self-expression."[3]

- Grace Kelly's father, John B. Kelly, was an outstanding oarsman who won an Olympic medal in 1920. But he was banned from the Henley regatta that same year because he was a bricklayer, not a gentleman. He was therefore not an "amateur" according to the understood rules of the game. Some decades earlier, half the oarsmen entered in a regatta on the Schuylkill River near Kelly's native Philadelphia had been banned because they were "not amateurs." By the ruling of the nominating committee, anyone who hoped to benefit financially from the regatta or competed for money was not an amateur—a definition that was ratified by a general meeting of rowing clubs in 1873. John Kelly, of course, earned a measure of revenge, since he made a fortune in the construction business and his daughter went on to become a princess. A road running along the Schuylkill River is now called "Kelly Drive."

• At the turn of the century tennis was a signature sport of wealth and leisure. Amateur tennis tournaments sponsored by organizations like the All-England Croquet and Lawn Tennis Club date from 1877, when the first Wimbledon Championship was held. The U.S. National Lawn Tennis Association was founded in 1881, and Australian, French, and Canadian amateur associations all developed within the next decade. Professional tennis began in 1926, and by the late 1940s the leading amateur champions were turning pro. In point of fact, the best players, while playing as amateurs, were already making a living from the game, since lesser tournaments had begun to pay them to show up and attract the crowds. In December 1967 the British Lawn Tennis Association unilaterally abolished the distinction between professional and amateur. A few proudly "amateur" events continued, like the Davis Cup, and some players resisted turning pro in order to represent their countries in such events. But by 1997, after years in which top United States players declined to compete, the U.S. Tennis Association was offering $100,000 to those who would agree to join the team.

- Popularized by the most celebrated "amateur" sports competition in the world, the Olympic Games, figure skating
has become a major viewer draw, rivaling pro football for
television ratings. It's difficult even for competitors to keep
the lines between professional and amateur straight.
Olympic gold medalist Tara Lipinski appeared in a show
called Skate, Rattle and Roll, and former world champion
Michelle Kwan in the U.S. Pro Championship. Both made
money for skating, but Lipinski is no longer allowed to
compete in Olympic or national championship events,
while Kwan is aiming for the 2002 Winter Olympics. As a
sports reporter observed, "In the world of figure skating,
it's more correct to say Lipinski is more pro than Kwan,
rather than to say Lipinski is a pro skater and Kwan is an
amateur." And skater Elvis Stojko's coach said simply,
"There doesn't seem to be much of a difference between
amateurs and pros these days. . . . You just about have to
be a Philadelphia lawyer to understand it."[4]

The founder of the modern Olympic Games, Baron Pierre de
Coubertin, insisted in 1894 that his international association
develop the spirit of amateur sport throughout the world.
New bylaws adopted in 1976, however, allowed athletes to
receive compensation while retaining their amateur status.
Permissible forms of compensation included personal sports
equipment and clothing, travel money, hotel expenses, and
payment for what was called "broken time"—that is, time that
would otherwise have been spent earning a living.[5] So a com-
petitor can in fact work full-time at his or her sport, while

retaining eligibility as an "amateur." This is a good paradigm case of the "professional amateur."

It may be worth noting that the amateur nature of the original games was to a certain extent Coubertin's fantasy. Athletes in ancient Greece received prizes for winning and substantial benefits from their home cities; they became full-time specialists, like their modern-day counterparts. The breakdown of the binary between amateur and professional was, that is to say, always (or even always already) present within the categories themselves.

"The line between professional and amateur sports is a joke," declared a sports and entertainment attorney. Amateur college athletes get free clothes from corporate sponsors. They practice not only the sanctioned twenty hours a week but another twenty "voluntary" hours (to get around National Collegiate Athletic Association guidelines). They have the use of student-athlete academic centers, financed by doting alumni and equipped with state-of-the-art computers and other amenities. As a national newspaper observed, noting the contract signed between a television network and the NCAA for the right to broadcast the annual men's college basketball tournament, "Amateurism has never been more lucrative."[6] In effect, these "amateurs" are professionals.

Let me point toward one further and familiar context—in addition to politics and sports—to frame this set of assumptions about amateur professionals and professional amateurs. For, as I hope is becoming increasingly clear, the two categories of amateur and professional, apparently distinct, are not only mutually enfolding but mutually constructed and mutually policed. My third context, one particularly beloved of college professors (perhaps because we like to think it's closer to what we do), is the world of classic detective fiction.[7]

Sherlock Holmes is a professional amateur who is an expert in a dozen obscure sciences and plays the violin, while his friend Watson is a medical doctor with an avocation as an amateur sleuth. Holmes, we are told, discovers his calling by chance when, while visiting the home of a college friend during the summer vacation, he performs some offhand feats of deduction and is advised, "That's your line of life, sir." Recalling the moment many years later, Holmes confides, "that recommendation . . . was, if you will believe me, Watson, the very first thing that made me feel that a profession might be made of what had up to that time been the merest hobby."[8] Holmes and Watson are in competition not so much with the criminals they pursue as with the police, in the person of the literal-minded and long-suffering Inspector Lestrade—the professional detective.

Agatha Christie's Miss Marple is not only an amateur but an "elderly amateur female sleuth," underestimated by professional crime solvers and by witnesses and victims. Her abject position (other characters in Christie novels often condescend to this little old lady with her balls of wool and her self-abnegating manner) is actually an excellent vantage point for observation (people expect old women to be snoops and gossips), and her modus operandi, the "village parallel" (reasoning by analogy), is paired with an unrelentingly low opinion of human nature. Miss Marple is an amateur professional.

Christie's other major detective, Hercule Poirot, is a retired officer of the Belgian Sûreté, also working free-lance, often in competition with the police, certainly not an amateur but also not simply a professional. With his Watson-like friend, the clueless Captain Hastings, he regularly outwits the authorities, and also protects his clients from unwanted publicity. Poirot is, in my terms, a professional amateur, in that he comes from a professional training but works as a free lance and for the pleasure of problem solving.

Mystery writer Dorothy L. Sayers offers a similar array of inspired amateurs, from the aristocratic Lord Peter Wimsey, whose hobbies, according to the stud-book, are incunabula and crime, to his protégée Miss Climpson, a middle-aged spinster whom he sets up as head of an unofficial detective agency composed entirely of women like herself—unmarried women who can quietly take up positions as secretaries, clerks, and paid companions and, virtually unnoticed by their employers, "detect" and investigate crimes. Wimsey's friend and brother-in-law Charles Parker is a middle-class Scotland Yard policeman with all the hallmarks of the professional: unimaginative, methodical, and dull.

Significantly, Poe's C. Augustus Dupin, the model for both Holmes and Poirot (and indeed, in a way, for Lord Peter), is explicitly a gentleman amateur and a collector: born "of an excellent, indeed of an illustrious family," fallen in material fortunes, but possessing "a small remnant of his patrimony," which he spends on books. "Books, indeed, were his sole luxuries." It is in fact in an "obscure library in the Rue Montmartre" that he first encounters his amanuensis and benefactor. They are both "in search of the same very rare and very remarkable volume" (which of course goes unnamed), and before too long they are sharing a mansion paid for by the narrator, who feels "that the society of such a man would be a treasure beyond price" and is "permitted to be at the expense of renting, and furnishing" a suitable dwelling. The two friends spend their time reading, writing, and conversing— the activities of leisured gentlemen—until Dupin's extraordinary analytical powers are put to the service of solving crimes. Again, Dupin's foil is the professional, the prefect of the Parisian police, who, like his men, fails because he considers only his own ideas of what is clever, and searches assiduously in all the obvious and conventional places.[9]

Dupin's aristocratic birth and mania for book collecting are symptomatic, for he is in fact a true descendant of the most honored tribe of amateurs, the virtuosi.

The Virtuoso, the Dilettante, and
the Public Intellectual

These days the word *virtuoso* has come to connote brilliance, ease, and perhaps a certain unseriousness. Like its more abjected companion, *dilettante*, it is associated with a kind of trifling or dabbling: the amusements of a rich man. (The normative virtuoso is still male, unless she is a musician or performer.) But in its original usage in the seventeenth century a "virtuoso" was not only a gentleman of leisure but also a learned person: a scholar, an antiquary, and a scientist.

Virtuosi were connoisseurs and collectors, gentlemen of wealth and leisure, identified with the aristocracy. Their interests ranged from painting and antiquities, coins and shells, to—increasingly, as the century wore on—"natural philosophy," or Renaissance science. The "virtuosi" were members of the Royal Society. But, it is crucial to note, their interest lay in the sheer pleasure of learning and the cultivation of reputation, whether for knowledge or for the possession of an enviable collection—not in what Francis Bacon would call "benefit and use."

The word virtuoso was first used in England in 1634, by Henry Peacham in his book on *The Compleat Gentleman,* to describe those who possessed rarities like classical statues, inscriptions, and coins: "Such as are skilled in them, are by the *Italians* termed *Virtuosi.*" The virtuoso blended the traditions of the courtier and the scholar, to become, precisely, a gentleman-scholar. He was not only an aristocrat; he was also, often, eager to distinguish himself from the "intruding upstart, shot up with last night's Mushroome" (the phrase again is Peacham's). There was a "snob appeal" to being an English virtuoso in the seventeenth century: you needed money, leisure, ancient family (Peacham's recipe for distancing yourself from the intruding upstarts was to study heraldry), intellectual curiosity, and someplace to store your collections, whether of shells, stones, coins, statues, or paintings. In the sixteenth century, the number of books owned by private individuals was, by modern standards, very small: except for clergy, only about a dozen members of the upper classes had more than a hundred.

In contrast, by the second half of the seventeenth century several country houses had rooms called libraries to accommodate their growing collections. And in addition to books, the gentry and the nobility began to collect and display paintings (not only portraits but landscapes, seascapes, and mythological paintings), sculpture and statuary, coins, gems, and medals, and what were called "curiosities": natural and manmade objects of interest from the remains of a dodo (collected and displayed by Elias Ashmole, the founder of the Ashmolean Museum) to the gloves of Edward the Confessor and "Henry VII's dog collar."[10] These collectors, and Ashmole foremost among them, were "virtuosi" or "virtuosos."

As Walter Houghton wrote more than fifty years ago, "we are misled by derogatory connotations which, in the course of time, got attached to 'virtuoso,' 'dilettante,' and 'amateur,' but which clearly did not belong to their primary and normal meanings; a 'dilettante' in the seventeenth century was still one who delighted—and it might be seriously—in learning and art."[11] The eighteenth century was a century of dilettantes. In 1733–34 the Society of Dilettanti was founded as an exclusive gentleman's club. Shortly thereafter Lord Chesterfield could characterize himself, however disingenuously, as a "humble dillettante" [*sic*] seeking information from a better-informed "virtuoso." But by 1886 John Ruskin was dismissing someone as a "mere dilettante."

To this historically interesting pair, the virtuoso and the dilettante, both borrowed from the Italian, we might add two more terms from European aesthetic culture that have come to connote amateur appreciation, the Spanish *aficionado* and, from the French *belles-lettres*, the *belletrist* or *bellettrist*, a devotee of the literary arts. *Aficionado* has its roots in *afición*, affection (just as *dilettante* comes from *delittare*, to delight), and began as a term for the enthusiasts of bullfighting. The aficionado, like the dilettante, is a "lover" or "amateur," though he, or she, need not be a practitioner. A dilettante painter paints; an aficionado of swing music may or may not ever wield the baton. *Aficionado* still carries the sense of the knowledgeable enthusiast, with a certain sense of elite pleasure or offbeat expertise, as in the name of an expensive fan magazine like *Cigar Aficionado*

Belles-lettres, the French term for "fine letters" or "literary studies," began as the equivalent for literature of *beaux arts*, "fine arts." In its early uses in the eighteenth century, *belles-lettres* was simply equivalent to literature or even the whole of the humanities. In Edinburgh and Glasgow, after the 1707 Act of Union between Scotland and England, professorships were founded in the new vernacular fields of "rhetoric and belles lettres," the forerunners of today's study of "English." Over the ensuing century, however, it became a term of vague disapprobation, something between appreciation and literary dabbling, especially when used as an adjective ("belletristic") or an adverb ("belletristically"). Matthew Arnold described himself, whether disingenuously or not, as "an unlearned belletristic trifler," and a nineteenth-century Oxford don wrote with satisfaction, in an account of his university's academic organization, "we have risen above the mere belletristic treatment of classical literature." By the 1920s literary critic John Middleton Murry was combining *dilettante* and *belles-lettres* in a consummate gesture of dismissal. "No amount of sedulous apery or word-mosaic," he wrote, "will make a writer of the dilettante bellettrist."[12] Today, although there is some nostalgia, at least among book reviewers and arts critics, for "what used to be called belles-lettres,"[13] as well as signs of resurgence of "literary appreciation" in college courses and scholarly books, the phase *belles-lettres* itself has pretty much vanished from academic use. Occasionally it surfaces in a journal or a magazine to describe gifted writers who might also be called virtuosi; thus a newspaper headline could characterize Gore Vidal and Norman Mailer as "boy toys of belles-lettres."[14]

In the United States, as in England, the gentlemanly amateur enjoyed a protracted ascendancy throughout the eighteenth and early nineteenth centuries. A good case in point, well documented by Timothy Duffy, was that of Charles Eliot Norton, businessman, essayist, social and literary reformer, Dante scholar, and ultimately professor of fine arts at Harvard University (1874–98).[15] The prestigious Norton Professorship of Poetry (significantly encompassing "together with Verse, all poetic expression in Language, Music, or the Fine Arts, under which term Architecture may be included") is named after him.[16] Norton in the antebellum period was an "amateur intellectual" in the best sense, participating in activities from political theory to social reform, then the typical sphere of women. He belonged to a number of clubs and literary associations, like the Saturday Club, the haunt of Emerson, Hawthorne, Holmes, and Longfellow. The Saturday Club at that time—and indeed until the second half of the twentieth century—did not admit woman members. The very *absence* of women allowed for the pursuit of sympathy and the expression of affectionate bonds between men. Charles Eliot Norton was a typical "amateur" of his time in his romantic same-sex correspondences with overseas friends like John

Ruskin, who professed himself jealous of Norton's fiancée, later his wife.

Norton's work on art history stressed moral lessons, the emotional power of medieval architecture, and the rewards of leisure, pleasure, and friendship. His Dante translations included passages of digression and personal reflection. Then came the Civil War, and with it an emphasis on "manliness." The blurred gender of gentlemanly work was increasingly precipitated out into male and female spheres. Amateurism was no longer in vogue. Pleasure and self-education, the amateur intellectual tradition, gave way to a desire for professional "work." Norton traveled in Europe in the 1860s and '70s, and when he returned, he asked his cousin, Charles W. Eliot, the president of Harvard, for a job. It would, he wrote to Eliot, "give me a definite status in the community, and this to a man of my age, without recognized profession, is of importance."[17] In 1874 Charles Eliot Norton was appointed professor of art history.

Norton's work changed. He began to add footnotes and technical notations to his formerly more sociable and personal translations of Dante. He wrote that no woman had ever produced first-rate poetry or works of imaginative literature. He criticized the "feminine passionateness" and "feminine susceptibility" of his male literary friends.[18] In short, the consummate "man of letters" had become a spokesman for "a more purely masculine definition of intellectual authority" and, in the process, had helped to separate what Duffy describes (paraphrasing Norton) as the "feminine dimensions of the life of letters" from the "organization of knowledge according to professional and objective standards."[19] That this attitude on the part of a professor of fine arts would redound against the prestige of the humanities was an ironic but perhaps inevitable result.

Not coincidentally, American higher education was itself in these years undergoing a similar makeover, moving away from the conversational and the personal toward "science," the specialization of knowledge, and a more "professional" notion of scholarship. Norton praised the founding of graduate schools, for example, because they would raise "the standard of professional learning and labour."[20] The word *amateur*, and its derogatory spin-off, *amateurish*, were increasingly terms of ill repute.[21] "Letters" and "literary" pursuits were associated with clubbiness and leisure, as well as with sentiment, gentility, and—inevitably—femininity and women.

And what *of* women? While men were creating a "professional" sphere that distinguished and protected their work from gentlemanly (and womanly) amateurishness, was the same divide between amateur and professional in force for women? Ann Douglas writes that in nineteenth-century America both ministers and women were "professionals masquerading as amateurs," pursuing careers rather than vocations.[22] Unsurprisingly, nineteenth-century women accomplished in the arts were admired if they were amateurs, but the word *professional* carried with it the hint, and the taint, of immorality—just as *pro* today, in policeman's slang, means "prostitute" (or, as we might translate it, "professional lover").

The sequence offered by a dictionary of slang is symptomatic:

Pro. 1. A professional in any field, as distinct from an amateur, and mainly distinguished by superior and dependable performance. 2. A seasoned and dependable performer; expert; model of excellence (also *old pro* or *real pro*). 3. A prostitute.

(As the dictionary speculates, the latter usage might come from "*professional* reinforced by *prostitute,* or vice versa."[23])

This doubleness—like the fact that in a number of languages "a public man" is a statesman while a "public woman" is a whore—tells us not only something about gender but also something about class, since it repeats, with some difference, the gentleman/amateur versus working-class/professional opposition we've seen in the history of sports.

It may be useful at this point to return to the specific terms of my topic, "The Amateur Professional and the Professional Amateur," to explore how these confusing terms might be different, and what difference that difference might make. My title takes the rhetorical form of a chiasmus, but these two crossing terms may threaten to collapse into an identity. What *is* an amateur professional? And what is a professional amateur? How are they different from one another? And why should it matter?

Provisionally, let us say that an *amateur professional* is someone who is learning, or poaching, or practicing without a license. The tyro; the amateur sleuth, whether of crime or of scholarship. Or, more recently and perhaps more pertinently, a person trained in one field who writes, thinks, practices, and publishes in another.

The *professional amateur,* by contrast, is someone who glories in amateur status. Often the professional amateur is *not* a professor, at least not one with a conventional academic training. If he or she *is* one, the odds are that some pains will be taken to disavow that fact. The dabbler, the dilettante, the virtuoso, the "man (or even "woman") of letters," the book reviewer, the belletrist, the polymath. And that current favorite, the "public intellectual."

The contemporary nostalgia for the category of the "public intellectual," the sense that some magic, synthetic moment of the recent past has been irretrievably lost, was exacerbated by the death of the "New York Intellectual" Alfred Kazin. Thomas Bender, a consistently thoughtful commentator on this question, has offered one of the best working definitions of "public intellectual" I've come across. Bender suggested that Kazin's accomplishments as a literary critic did not themselves suffice to make him a public intellectual. It was rather what he used literature *for.* "He used literature for larger purposes, to talk about subjects that mattered to contemporary society. His capacity to speak to more general and deeply felt worries, questions and aspirations, and to do so in a common idiom, made him a public intellectual."[24] Obituaries loved to dwell on the serendipity of Kazin's career; the story of his reading a book review on the subway, storming off the train in Times Square to confront the *Times* book review editor about it, and promptly being offered a job. This is the stuff of which legends are made. Kazin, we were reminded, wrote for magazines and newspapers, reviewed books for a living, and made the Reading Room of the New York Public Library his "home office." He belonged to the natural aristocracy of letters, achieved by merit, not by birth.[25] Although in his later years he taught at universities, he was not that now despised thing, "an academic." Rather, he was forged in the working-house of thought of New York City, following in the footsteps of older (and WASPier) critics and intellectuals like Edmund Wilson, Dwight Macdonald, Lewis Mumford, and Malcolm Cowley.

What I want to stress here is the degree to which these "intellectuals" were, and still are, celebrated for their professional amateurism. It has become, in effect, a sign of realness, what I'd call an "authenticity effect."

Hence the present-day nostalgia for Edmund Wilson and Kenneth Burke. Burke never completed college or took a degree. He was the music critic of the *Dial* and the *Nation* before turning to the field of literary criticism. He lectured at the University of Chicago for a couple of years, taught at Bennington, and held visiting professorships and lecture-ships in the United States and Europe, but he wasn't a "college professor" in the ordinary sense of the term. Likewise, critics and editors like Mumford, Macdonald, and Wilson wrote essays, book reviews, journal articles, opinion, and polemic. They didn't have university positions. They seem to have been free-standing, not tied to an institution, although the periodicals they edited were supported and sustained by institutions just as empowering as any professor's bully-podium.

The nostalgia for these "last" or "lost" intellectuals is, like all nostalgias, produced retrospectively and structured like a fantasy. Its genius is that it brings together the mystique of amateurism with the grittiness of the self-made man, thus

magically banishing any taint of (a) hereditary privilege and
(b) femaleness or femininity. Thus, this nostalgia solves an
image problem: how to conceive of a literary intellectual, a
"man of letters," as a man.

It is interesting to note that complaints against the so-
called "academic star system" of the 1980s and '90s also
break along the fault lines of professional amateur and amateur professional. When professors of the humanities and social sciences make headlines, it is often because someone
thinks their salaries or lecture fees are too high. A star economics professor's negotiations with two top Ivy League institutions were featured in the financial pages of the *New York
Times*. Literary scholar Stanley Fish was described as "the fin-
est example" of academics following the commercial model,
since he "once wrote an essay in which he described the pleasure he had in tooling around campus in his expensive sports
car." An article in a major newspaper commenced with delib-
erate provocation, "Speaking fees. Are they academia's dirty
little secret?" But as a piece in the *Chronicle of Higher Education*
reported, the luminaries brought to campus by student
groups and compensated with five-figure speaking fees tend
to be media celebrities, sports stars, talking heads, and politicians, rather than academics.[26] Nonetheless, in the public eye
an "academic superstar" is often seen as a contradiction in
terms. The phrase itself, now common in newspaper parlance, tells a story of commercialization and glitz. On the
"love or money" scale (amateur vs. professional), such stars
are seen to be in it for what they can get. They are poster
professors—how can they also be "lovers" of literature, or art,
or whatever it is they profess?

Perhaps the ultimate in professional-amateur training is the new, Ph.D.-granting "Public Intellectuals Program" at Florida Atlantic University in Boca Raton. The president of the university declared in the program's brochure that this degree in comparative studies will "help tomorrow's public intellectuals find their path," combining, he said in a flourish of humanist nostalgia, "the *vita contemplativa* with the *vita activa.*" Designed by feminist critic Teresa Brennan, the curriculum of the PIP offers courses in ethnic conflict, technology, feminism, environmentalism, and (of course) the power of the media. It is significant that Brennan felt called upon to assure potential detractors that "this is not an anti-intellectual program."[27] But despite the program's merits, at least one skeptic doubted that "the Boca Raton intellectuals" would ever become a phrase to conjure with. The area codes of what he dubbed "publicity intellectuals" needed to be closer to New York, he thought, since "culture editors don't take the time to delve too deeply into academe."[28]

Professional amateurs? Amateur professionals? Where the New York Intellectuals are seen—looking backward in time from a rose-colored distance—to have been somehow above the fray while in the thick of it, professors who "cross over" from academia to the public realm are subject, precisely, to a critique of their genuineness.

It may not always be possible to distinguish the amateur professional from the professional amateur. These are analytic categories, not transcendent truths, and I am introducing them precisely because they pose the problems of "difference within" that they do. But—and this is a key point—the degree to which individuals succeed in identifying themselves as the one or the other has a great deal to do with how seriously, and pleasurably, they are taken.

Getting Down to Cases

Here, then, are a few symptomatic examples.

- The success of a cultural icon like Sister Wendy, the nun who has "emerged from behind monastery walls" to become "the most unlikely and famous television art critic of our time,"[29] was predicated to a certain extent upon the romance of her "amateur" status. Discovered after she appeared in a BBC program on the National Gallery, Sister Wendy Beckett, with her trailing habit and her toothy smile, soon became a popular sensation. The apparent paradox (or titillating nonparadox) of a celibate nun in her sixties offering frank and admiring appraisals of sexual moments in great art, when combined with her straightforward, nonspecialist language, made for strong media appeal. One network official, seeing the original broadcast, remarked to his colleagues, "The only one we understood was Sister Wendy. Give her a series." In Sister Wendy we have a member of a religious order who is celebrated, precisely, for her lay status, her amateur professionalism in the world of art.

- Oprah Winfrey's status as arbiter of public literary taste was teasingly addressed by former *New York Times Book Review* editor Rebecca Pepper Sinkler in a piece called "My Case of Oprah Envy." Goaded by Alfred Kazin's grumpy description of Oprah's Book Club as "the carpet bombing of the American mind," and wondering whether she herself had retired "just before Winfrey's new TV book club would put all my colleagues in the lit crit industry out of work," Sinkler did the bold thing: she called Oprah and asked her. Turns out that, so far from wanting to usurp the role of book reviewers, Oprah depends on them, reading book review sections and looking for books that appeal to her. She sees herself as an advocate, rather than an "impartial" reviewer.

Oprah can make her own rules. Although she keeps the identity of a chosen book secret from the viewing public till the day the show airs, the authors and publishers are notified, wined and dined, and wafted to Chicago, where they appear on *Oprah!* with their hostess and hear her urge her viewers to "Buy the book!" And millions do. As Sinkler noted, "In marked contrast to rave reviews by keepers of the cultural flame, Winfrey's word moves the mass market."[30] In recognition, the National Book Awards ("the literary version of the Oscars") presented her with its fiftieth-anniversary gold medal, stressing that the medal was "being given for a literary reason, not a marketing reason," because Oprah "raises the cultural values of America."[31] Who is Oprah Winfrey that she should have such power? Well, she's Oprah Winfrey.

Both of these examples—and I admit that they are, deliberately, both spectacular and tendentious ones—are *women* who have gained some authority in the *arts*. That one is a nun and the other an African American only underscores the degree to which outsider status may actually undercut the fear of women. These are "exceptional" women in more than one sense. They are coded as "amateur professionals"— reaching over into a world of expertise centered in the humanities.

But, as we might perhaps expect, much of the action these days is on the frontier between the humanities and the sciences.

The word *scientist* was in fact coined on the model of *artist* in the 1830s, after the members of the British Association for the Advancement of Science had "felt very oppressively" the absence of such a term: "*Philosophers* was felt to be too wide and too lofty . . . ; *savans* was rather assuming . . . ; some ingenious gentleman proposed that, by analogy with *artist,* they might form *scientist,* and added that there could be no scruple in making free with this termination [-*ist*] when we have such words as *sciolist, economist,* and *atheist*—but this was not generally palatable."[32] A *sciolist* is a pretentious know-it-all; these are not, any of them, neutral analogies. The tone of this nineteenth-century account is both droll and witty.

So in linguistic terms *scientist* is a back formation from *artist,* just as *heterosexual* is a back formation from *homosexual.* In both cases the general category of analysis (knowledge, sexuality) comes under scrutiny, and the result is a pair of opposed terms, developed in relation to one another, where the one coined second is treated as if it had been coined first.

Here it may be well to remind ourselves that in the course of the nineteenth century, "science" had only gradually come to mean physical and experimental science rather than theology and metaphysics, and that the consequent division of knowledge had a class component at the universities, where a classical education, the traditional education of a gentleman amateur, still outranked the vocational connotations of practical science. We might compare this with the supposed "uselessness" of a liberal arts degree today.

The lack of symmetry between professional and amateur, and between "male" and "female," leads to some interesting developments on this borderline between scientist and artist.

One telling example is that fascinating midcentury figure C. P. Snow. Trained as a research scientist in the field of infrared spectroscopy at Cambridge's celebrated Cavendish Laboratory, Snow, at the age of twenty-five, was elected a fellow of Christ's College and seemed headed for a successful research career, until an awkward error—the announcement of a scientific breakthrough that then had to be recanted—led to his withdrawal from the research labs. Although he retained his scientific fellowship until 1945, the coiner of the phrase "the two cultures"[33] moved firmly and inexorably into the second, becoming a popular novelist and playwright, the author of the eleven "Strangers and Brothers" novels, and a controversial public figure and pundit. Snow's critique of F. R. Leavis and others he dismissed as "literary intellectuals" was proffered by a writer best known at the time not as a scientist, but as a novelist who published middle-brow fiction about science. Leavis in turn lambasted Snow as someone who only "thinks of himself as a novelist" but who is, in fact, a very bad writer indeed, and moreover someone who doesn't understand the very realm—academia—about which he has chosen to write.[34]

Snow, we could say, was a professional who became a professional amateur. It was his "amateur" status, as well as his history of professionalism in another venue, that gave him the authority to pontificate. Yet as a scion of the upwardly striving lower-middle class he attacked what he called "the traditional culture" (which he associated with gentlemen, literati, humanists and amateurs) on behalf of the rising "new class" of scientists, policy-makers and technocrats. In other words, professionals.

Consider now the case of naturalist E. O. Wilson, a two-time Pulitzer Prize winner (for *On Human Nature* and *The Ants*), who wrote a book called *Consilience: The Unity of Knowledge*. In *Consilience*, Wilson urged a return to the holistic view of knowledge, from molecular biology through ethics and theology, and embracing all the natural and social sciences, the arts and humanities.[35] The word "consilience," meaning "the jumbling together of knowledge from different disciplines," was coined in 1840 by William Whewell, the man who is said by some to have coined the word "scientist." Wilson's book was both praised as "an act of consummate intellectual heroism" and dismissed as "a narrow Procrustean bed of reductionism." According to Wilson, "The central idea of consilience" was that "all tangible phenomena . . . are reducible to the laws of physics." Thus, though many modes of knowledge could be combined, there was a hierarchy among intellectuals, with the scientist, perhaps unsurprisingly, at the top. Interviews with the genial and telegenic author appeared in numerous media outlets. He was described as "a towering figure in the study of the nature of human nature," and criticisms of his earlier book *Sociobiology* were dismissed as misunderstandings or the carpings of the "radical left."[36]

But some readers took issue with the very premise of *Consilience*, as well as with Wilson's evidently limited views on cubism, genetics, and modern architecture. "It encourages us to see unity ahead of the evidence, to force the facts of observations into an arbitrary mould," said one. "And it invites specialists whose training has equipped them for a fairly narrow scientific niche to stray into fields for which they are ill-adapted."[37] The key point was, once again, the tension between generalist and specialist. "The central problems of art seem to have escaped Wilson's attention," wrote literary critic Tzvetan Todorov, arguing that "Wilson seeks not to reconcile the natural sciences and the social sciences, but to facilitate the absorption of the latter by the former and also to cede to the biological glutton the meaning of the creative arts and the direction of our moral and political actions."[38] Did Wilson's professional identity as a man of science (and a Pulitzer Prize winner) entitle him to generalize about all human knowledge and human nature? Had he earned the right to be a professional amateur?

Another scientist who has traveled far from his disciplinary home is Carl Djerassi, a chemist who played an important role in the development of the birth control pill. In his late twenties Djerassi was awarded a National Medal of Science and the Priestly Medal, the highest award given Americans for work in chemistry. He bought stock in Syntex, the "pill" company, gained control of it, and became a rich man. For a variety of reasons, both personal and intellectual, Djerassi began to write novels and, later, plays. Now he describes himself as an "intellectual polygamist." The only thing that keeps him awake at night, he says, is "a vicious review."[39]

Significantly, one admiring account of a Djerassi play called it "not the creation of a fiction writer playing casually with a hot topic" but "real science, from the pen of a man who knows it well."[40] In other words, Djerassi's accomplishments as a professional chemist gave him authority and cachet as a writer. "Scientists don't read much fiction," says Djerassi, explaining why he feels somewhat estranged from both the literary and the scientific communities. "They think I have just given up on their field. The literary people look at me as a scientist who is now trying to hobnob. They make cracks like, 'Gee, maybe I should go into the lab for a couple of years and see what kind of chemistry I can do.' But I couldn't have written my fiction if I didn't steep myself in the scientific culture for my entire adult life."[41]

So according to Carl Djerassi, as to C. P. Snow and E. O. Wilson, it is possible to go from a career in science to one in the arts. Scientists like Stephen Jay Gould, Richard Dawkins, and Stephen Hawking may well be regarded as a new genre of professional amateurs or "public intellectuals." But can one go in the other direction? I'd say the jury is still out. Here are a pair of examples that may (or may not) seem to point in opposite directions.

Literary critic Elaine Scarry, a professor of English, published a long article in the *New York Review of Books* suggesting that the crash of TWA flight 800 was caused by electromagnetic interference, perhaps from military craft flying or floating in the area. The *Boston Globe* treated her outsider status with gingerly respect: "Scarry, though without personal expertise in technology or electromagnetic systems, has written on health and medicine."[42] Wire service reports led off with the surprising nonfit between her job and the argument she was making ("'A Harvard University English professor believes . . .").[43] Scarry herself was quoted as telling a reporter that her interest in electromagnetic interference fit into "her academic specialty—cross-disciplinary studies, which she described as 'looking at certain questions to see how they occur across different fields or disciplines,' such as law, medicine, and science."[44] An extremely polite and even courtly exchange of letters between Scarry and James Hall, chair of the National Transportation Safety Board, was published in the *NYRB*, in which she said it was an honor to be in correspondence with him and he said he would get right onto this.

Scarry was in this case clearly writing as an amateur professional, not a professional amateur. She had done her homework, as the voluminous footnotes attested. She wanted to be taken seriously as someone who could speak science. It wasn't "love" but moral and political urgency that motivated her argument. And yet there were skeptics who wondered what standing she could possibly have in this matter.

The disequilibrium between science and literature was well illustrated by the now-notorious Sokal affair, in which a physicist submitted an article full of high-sounding nonsense to the unsuspecting editors of *Social Text*. The editors bought the parody, and were exposed, gleefully, in *Lingua Franca: The Review of Academic Life*. Alan Sokal and his Belgian coauthor, Jean Bricmont, proceeded to write a book, *Fashionable Nonsense: Postmodern Intellectuals' Abuse of Science*, in which they claimed to be exposing an even bigger hoax: the misuse of scientific terms and paradigms by French theorists like Jacques Lacan, Julia Kristeva, and Deleuze and Guattari.

Of the many things that could be said about this risible, irritating, and self-important event, I want to restrict myself to one: the observation that humanists playing with scientific terms and concepts are often seen as less noble, and more ridiculous, than scientists playing with cubism and theology. Scientist E. O. Wilson was a consummate intellectual hero— or at least a sanctioned amateur professional, whose broadest and most "humanist" pronouncements (and TV appearances) qualified him also for professional amateur (or "pundit") status. Steven Weinberg, winner of a Nobel Prize for his work in particle physics, also received the Lewis Thomas Prize, awarded to the researcher who best embodies "the scientist as poet." It is difficult today to imagine a major prize for the obverse talent, the embodiment of "the poet as scientist."[45] Humanist intellectuals like Lacan, Kristeva, and Luce Irigaray are not regarded as provocative readers of science but as imposters, spouters of "fashionable nonsense." The split between amateurs and professionals reproduces itself in the relative standing of fields: scientists can become humanists more easily than humanists scientists, in part because the humanities themselves are perceived as closer to "love" than is science.

The Academic and the Journalist

It's notable that most of the figures I have cited above, including those who earn their living as university professors, came to public attention not through their scholarship but through the media, and especially through journalism and network television. One of the things professional amateurs do these days is have comfy chats with Charlie Rose. Why, then, is *journalistic* such a dirty word in academic circles, and *academic* such a term of opprobrium among journalists? In each case, there is almost no worse thing you can say. Each is the abject of the other.

The truly divided "two cultures" of our time may prove to be not, as C. P. Snow initially suggested, the humanities and the sciences—now approaching one of their periodic rapprochements, through the humanistic fascination with evolutionary psychology, fractals, cybernetics and the history of science on the one hand and the popular prestige of "the scientist as poet" on the other—but rather journalism and academia. The fact that the former group is populated to a certain extent by disaffected members of the latter, and that the latter secretly aspires to be as "mainstream" as the former, only exacerbates the periodic tension between the two.

For a scholar to describe a scholarly book as "journalistic" is to say that it lacks hard analysis, complexity, or deep thought. For a journalist to describe a scholarly book as "academic" is to say that it is abstruse, dull, hard to read, and probably not worth the trouble of getting through. Yet in their heart of hearts, scholars long for public and even popular recognition. The Holy Grail of the "crossover book," one that impresses one's colleagues but also appeals to the intelligent general reader and perhaps even makes the best-seller list, is a recurring dream in the profession. And in their heart of hearts, for all I know, journalists may long to teach courses at a university and do months of research in libraries and archives. Certainly many journalists avail themselves of sabbatical opportunities to spend time on university campuses as fellows or visiting scholars, and many science reporters pursue in depth the subjects they touch on in their columns. Yet as in Snow's famous description, the journalist and the scholar sometimes seem divided by "a gulf of mutual incomprehension."[46] Where then did things go wrong between them?

In part this is merely a matter of the differentiation between neighboring fields, the overestimation of what distinguishes them—what Sigmund Freud memorably termed "the narcissism of minor differences." But the tension between journalism and academia also has to do with the very different goals of the two kinds of writing—goals that are misunderstood when they are described merely in terms of simplicity and complexity, or clarity and difficulty. It is not that journalists write in a style that is simple and clear (though some do) and that scholars write in a style that is complex and difficult (though some do). Some journalists use complex language, and some scholars' writing is both simple and clear (which does not necessarily mean that it is readily comprehensible to someone outside the field). The difference is rather that the journalist of ideas attempts to explain and describe them, while the scholar of ideas attempts to think through them, to enter into and advance an ongoing intellectual discussion. Every scholarly move is part of a dialogue. To hear only one side of the conversation and take it for the whole is almost inevitably to find the current speaker's contribution unaccountable, dogmatic, or slightly ridiculous.

A telling case in point here is the "Arts & Ideas" section in the Saturday *New York Times*. The columnists engaged in this brave venture have set themselves a daunting task, since one of the most difficult of intellectual challenges is to decribe a complex concept in terms simple enough for the layperson to understand. All too often such simplifications run the risk of losing the very nuances and counterintuitive implications that make the original idea important and valuable. Thus, for example, I can read accounts of paleontology or string theory, topics about which I know nothing, and come away from them feeling (perhaps quite falsely) well informed. I don't know enough to know where the popular account may have gone wrong. But when an article sets out to explain something I do know about, something perhaps basic to my own work, I often feel frustrated by the writer's flattening-out of three-dimensional ideas. It may be a question of genre: what is lost in translation between academia and journalism is of particular interest (only) to people working in the field itself.

This is partly a matter of how many "bounces" you can allow an idea to have. The "one-bounce" idea is appealing but often false. "Deconstruction is nihilistic." But hot-button words like this are what I might call "two-" or even "three-bounce" topics, which require an intellectual set-up in order to seem anything but foolish or willfully perverse. It is often said, for instance, that deconstruction does not "believe" in truth. But if deconstruction were to *affirm* that truth does not exist, then that statement would pretend to know the truth about truth, and thus be an *example* of the very thing deconstruction questions. Media accounts of deconstruction always attribute *negative* certainties to it, rather than describing deconstruction as analytical work performed upon the very *possibility* of statements of certainty as such, whether positive or negative.

One of the strategies initially adopted by the Arts & Ideas page was what might be termed prophylactic, protecting or guarding its readers against too unmediated an encounter with scholars. Thus, for example, a promotional newsletter distributed to *Times* subscribers promised them a steady source of information about "The (Next) Big Idea" in academic life but was careful to put distance between the *Times*'s own lively reports and boring scholarship. "You won't find the word 'scholar' in any of our headlines," it promised.[47]

Another strategy might be described as ethnographic, since it consists of articles describing the strange folk and stranger folkways of that curious land called "academia." The most exuberant of these articles fall roughly into two types, the celebrity interview and the silly-trendy-conference-and-research-field. The celebrity interview often has a cozy culinary component, the identifying mark of "genuineness" in journalistic accounts. Thus we find lead sentences like "Jacques Derrida, perhaps the world's most famous philosopher—if not the only famous philosopher—was eating barbecued chicken with a knife and fork at the Polo Grill."[48] Or, "[Eve Kosofsky] Sedgwick, 47, was sitting in the shadows at a restaurant in midtown Manhattan and trying to explain 'queer theory,' the academic field she has helped create."[49] Sometimes the humanizing detail is sartorial: "the amiable

[Stephen Jay] Gould, with a pair of glasses hung around his neck, hit upon Karl Marx's funeral . . . the year 2000 . . . and Yogi Berra's wisdom, before finally alighting on his thesis: that people, especially scientists, are terrible at predicting the future."[50]

As for articles in the spirit of "What'll they think of next to waste your tax dollars and your kids' tuition money on?" these seem largely gleaned from old Modern Language Association programs and announcements of future conferences. I recall one article that seemed to be entirely based on conversations with scholars who hadn't yet given their papers but had announced their paper titles, and had been contacted—and elevated to A&I "queen for a day" status—on the basis of this promise of future work. There was the "Martha Stewart studies" article and the "shopping studies" article and the "millennial studies" article.[51] In response to such articles it might be said that the risk of appearing absurd at times is necessary to the scholarly enterprise. If scholars always stayed within the bounds of prudence and common sense, many original ideas would be lost.

There are several models for the *Times* A&I page. One is the MLA program and the annual joke articles derived from it; a second is the eighties wave of "aren't they silly" tenured-radical books by critics of the state of academia; and the third, a more serious interrogator of the profession and its foibles, is *Lingua Franca.* Founded in 1990 as (in its own words) "a lively, engaging magazine about academic life—the working conditions and prominent personalities, the theory jousting and administrative maneuvering, plus news about tenure appointments and the business of academic publishing,"[52] *Lingua Franca* filled a market niche whose existence many might have doubted. Described by its editor as "the best bathroom reading" a humanities junkie will ever find, *Lingua Franca* aimed, curiously enough, to broaden the views of the same "narrow specialists" targeted by critics of the academy. "Given the structure of the academic world, most people are forced to specialize in very narrow areas," said publisher Jeffrey Kittay. "We're trying to give academics exposure to all the interesting stuff out there so they won't feel so pigeonholed," added another editor.[53] Skeptics assumed that the general public would stay away in droves, but the magazine prospered (to the extent that magazines do), winning a number of awards, publishing a tell-all guide to graduate programs, and profiling both celebrity professors (Slavoj Žižek, Elaine Showalter) and academic obsessions (body building, fashion, jazz: "The word outside the academy," read one symptomatic pull-quote, "is that jazz is too important to leave to academics").[54]

Lingua Franca was, indeed, almost irresistibly readable. It was "the *People* magazine of Academia," one staff writer told the *Washington Post*, and was devoured the same way, "on the sly and with great pleasure and guilt."[55] Alumni and alumnae of its editorial staff found their way into mainstream magazine publishing, and also into the world of book reviewing. Newspapers began to pick up the sillier snippets within even serious pieces and recycle them as sure-fire laugh lines, reinventing that old favorite, the "absentminded professor," as his spectral opposite, what might be called the "presentminded professor," a creature so concerned with wardrobe, "trendiness," and academic style that real scholarship was sure to be left behind.

It's not without interest that once again the crossover was only seen as legitimate in one direction. For a journal about academics to resemble *People* was new and ground-breaking. For MLA president Elaine Showalter actually to write for *People* earned her scorn in a number of quarters, not excepting (you guessed it) *Lingua Franca.*

Headers and Footers

The slippery borderline between being too professional and being too amateur can also be traced to something as simple and as telling as the status of the footnote. In his feisty polemic about the Modern Language Association, *The Fruits of the MLA* (published in the fateful year 1968), Edmund Wilson attacked the pedantry of scholarly editions of literary classics, which (he claimed) took the pleasure out of reading. Extensive footnotes, variants, canceled passages, and erasures spoiled the reader's pleasure in the text. Wilson's friend Lewis Mumford had compared footnote numbers and other apparatus in the text to "barbed wire" keeping the reader at arm's length. Wilson concurred, ridiculing the 89 pages of introductory material and 143 pages of notes that accompanied a scholarly edition of *The Marble Faun* ("This information is of no interest whatever"). Wilson mocked the professors who were reading Tom Sawyer backward, in the spirit of the Hinman Collating Machine, so as to be able to track textual variants without being distracted by the plot or the style. The professionals had ruined the experience of reading for pleasure.

Gordon Ray, president of the Guggenheim Foundation, responded (in the preface to an MLA booklet called *Professional Standards: A Response to Edmund Wilson*) by noting that Wilson's critique "derives in part from the alarm of amateurs at seeing rigorous professional standards applied to a subject in which they have a vested interest." Ray saw such tensions in "field after field from botany to folklore" and concluded, "In the long run professional standards always prevail."[56] The battle between professionals and amateurs had (again) been joined.

The shibboleth of the footnote—a footnote fetish, if you will—has continued to be a marker of the professional/amateur divide. Newspaper and magazine journalists, of course, never use them. Instead they use "fact checkers" behind the scenes and—by the dexterous employment of these dedicated offstage professionals—keep their own writing pristine and unadorned. This creates what we might call "the knowledge effect": by erasing any trace of informants or sources, oral or written, the journalist seems self-sufficient, all-knowing, independent and whole. On the other hand, among scholars in many disciplines, footnote citation indexes are used as a measure of comparative value. The more you are cited, the greater your influence. "In the marketplace of ideas," says Jon Wiener, "the footnote is the unit of currency." As a result "citation indexing becomes a basis for promotion and tenure, for grants and fellowships."[57] So both footnotes and their absence can produce the knowledge effect, depending upon the genre. And in some humanities fields scholars can be measured by the size of their footnotes—the mark of professional display.

In an article called "Where Have All the Footnotes Gone?"[58] first published in the *New York Times Book Review*, historian Gertrude Himmelfarb lamented the sorry state of footnote practice in the field of history and also in the publishing business more generally. A growing number of scholarly books, she noted, "have no notes at all, [and] even pride themselves on their lack of notes." Urged on by publishers with crass commercial motives, who want to "make scholarly books look more accessible and thus more marketable," some eager authors, scenting royalties, have acquiesced in this practice, "hoping to attract innocent readers by hiding the scholarly paraphernalia." Himmelfarb deplores the endnote, which banishes the note material to the back of the book, creating an uncomfortable experience for the reader and, worse, a "demoralizing effect on the author," who soon begins to exhibit laxity in footnote form, then laxity in footnote content, and finally, in a total capitulation to fallen standards, lapses into "contempt for any kind of notes, ultimately dispensing with them altogether."

Despite my tone here, which mirrors Himmelfarb's rather playful, if also heartfelt, prose, and despite the fact that she and I might not see eye to eye on some questions of politics and culture, I agree with almost everything she says about footnote loss. But I have also observed the undeniable fact that in some disciplines—literary criticism, for example—the absence of footnotes is a bold, in-your-face declaration of pro-

fessional amateurism in its most magisterial form. The book
without footnotes trumps the merely "academic," footnoted
book, transcending ordinary scholarship and the presumed
"political" or "careerist" or "specialist" concerns of professionals.

Learning from a Pro

A suggestive case in point is Harold Bloom's book *Shakespeare:
The Invention of the Human,* one of the few genuinely successful crossover books of our time. The book was described by
New York Times theater critic Mel Gussow as "dutifully unschol-
arly, with no footnotes and not even an index." It's a book
intended "to be useful to common readers and common
playgoers," said its author, who described himself as a "pure
esthete," as distinct from the "hideous ideologues" who in-
habit present-day academia. "I don't want a single person,
with a few honorable exceptions, who ostensibly teach Shakespeare to even look at the book," he told Gussow.[59] It is striking, however, that his publishers were betting, or wishing, the
other way, paying for a full-page ad on the inside cover of
the PMLA program, a publication read almost exclusively by
professors and graduate students of literature.

Harold Bloom is a theorist I greatly admire. I was his col-
league (though not his student), and he is for me a valued
"old acquaintance" (a phrase he would recognize—it's
Prince Hal describing Falstaff). I don't take issue with his
book, which I read and enjoyed, but rather with the two

claims, reported in Gussow's article, that (1) someone interested in political and philosophical criticism of Shakespeare's plays can't also be a "pure esthete," and (2) that the way to demonstrate such purity is to omit any scholarly apparatus, including an index.

This kind of approach to Shakespeare is not, of course, without precedent. In the first part of the twentieth century, overt and determined protestations of amateurism by literary scholars set a certain gentlemanly tone. For reasons that may have to do with popular notions about the universal humanity of the author, these protestations seem particularly in evidence when the topic is Shakespeare. "Ladies and Gentlemen: I am no Shakespearian scholar, and if I have ventured, at the invitation of the Academy, to accept the perilous honor of delivering its Annual Shakespeare Lecture in succession to lecturers, and in the presence of listeners, whose authority on this subject is far greater than mine, it is for a definite reason." So classical scholar Gilbert Murray, the Regius Professor of Greek at Oxford, commenced his remarks on "Hamlet and Orestes" before the British Academy in 1914.

"A critic who makes no claim to be a true Shakespearian scholar and who has been honored by an invitation to speak about Shakespeare to such an audience as this, feels rather like a child brought in at dessert to recite his piece before the grown-ups," began novelist, medievalist, and Christian essayist C. S. Lewis when he addressed the same body in 1942. "The method is completely open, unprofessional, unassuming," writes John Bayley in praise of Oxford Professor of Poetry A. C. Bradley's famous lectures on Shakespearean tragedy, first published in 1904. "He talks about Shakespeare and Shakespeare's characters as if he were discussing friends or colleagues, or the people he has met with in a memorable novel."

Something of this magisterial "unprofessionalism" informs Bloom's views of Shakespeare. But it marks as much of a change from his early intellectual style as he himself once proudly differed from the Oxford dons, the Yale mandarins, and, in his own phrase, the "neo-Christian cabal" of T. S. Eliot and the New Critics.[60]

Bloom is, of course, a master of self-reinvention. To see just what this entails, let's go back a little in history.

Starting in 1973, Harold Bloom, who had begun as a scholar of rebellious Romantic poets like Shelley and Blake, published a series of studies of English poetry in which he argued, compellingly and complexly, that all strong poets rebel against their precursors by rewriting them. The relation between one poet and another could be described through certain "revisionary ratios," which Bloom denoted, deliberately, by uncommon words with Latin or Greek roots: *clinamen, tessera, kenosis, daemonization, askesis,* and *apophades.*[61] The younger Bloom was—though he liked to deny it—an important member of what was referred to as "the Yale School," and his writing style was dense with literary allusions and difficult terms.

Jerome McGann observed more than twenty years ago that the obscurity of Bloom's prose displayed "rhetorical conventions [that] seem to be the common property of a small club whose only permanent member is Bloom himself."[62] Elizabeth Bruss, in a largely admiring analysis of Bloom's achievement in "writing theory as a form of literature," noted his "thickly encrusted allusions" to fellow Yale professors Geoffrey Hartman, J. Hillis Miller, and Paul de Man.[63] Bruss points out that in *A Map of Misreading*, which Bloom published in 1975, the revisionary ratios "become notoriously difficult to apply. In fact, they are (perversely, but one suspects deliberately), both ill-defined and over-defined."[64] Bruss astutely characterizes both the historical moment and the critic's dilemma, for in this period, the early and midseventies, there was in literary studies

> a highly charged atmosphere of competing schools and credos, of rapid accelerations and more-avant-garde-than-thou positions wherein the wrong allusion, a misplaced phrase, or a taboo word can expose one to contemptuous dismissal or charges of heresy. The overlay of citations and qualifications, the code words that fill so many recent essays (and not Bloom's alone) are a function of this need for prominently displaying one's sophistication. In such an atmosphere and amid such obvious evidence of intimidation and vested power, it [was] difficult for Bloom . . . to assume [his] former posture as [a] rebellious outsider. . . . [He] lived to see his own most cherished subversions become the elements of a new orthodoxy—an awkward circumstance that may have helped to push [him] toward greater extravagance and, ultimately, into adopting a new kind of theoretical discourse with a more ambiguously fictive status.[65]

The fiction to which she refers is Bloom's "gnostic fantasy," *The Flight to Lucifer*, published in 1976.[66] But ultimately he chose a different path, rejecting his disciples by embracing his sometimes distant and dead precursors, and, in a gesture of willed and scornful disinheritance, by refusing to read those now middle-aged critics who had profited from reading him. The stage of "*daemonization*" ("to generalize away the uniqueness of the earlier work") was easier to achieve when the "earlier" work was, to use another Bloomian term, "belated"—when those critics he was responding to were, in fact, his own students, stepstudents, or grandstudents. The author of *The Anxiety of Influence*, which taught the (Oedipal) necessity of "swerving" from the path of prior giants, is now "swerving" from his *own* priority, excoriating current-day intellectuals for exactly the kinds of coinages, allusions, citations, and critical density that once marked his own prose.

What is zealously preserved in Bloom's rejection of footnotes and scholars is a certain attitude. "Rebelliousness" and "outsider" status are retained, as is even a measure of "subversiveness," now put to the service of pathos. His own terminology can be set aside, since it is now seen to interfere with "pure" aesthetic response or connoisseurship. Instead of Bloom the romantic Young Turk, tilting at the Establishment, we have Bloom as Falstaff, upbraiding the cold and calculating Prince Hals of a successor generation. If younger scholars, following Bloom's own example, coin or borrow terms from philosophy and rhetoric, he will decry them as technocrats and fakers and write instead in the magisterial and humanistic language of the predecessors against whom he once led the charge.

In short, Bloom has performed a perfectly and brilliantly "Bloomian" act, taking himself—his former self—as the

strong precursor. He will be both enfant terrible and émi-
nence grise. Like Bottom, he will play all the parts.

Bloom does amateurism like an old pro. It's the tran-
sumption of his old self that produces the most empowered
amateur.

This is a virtuoso move.

What's Love Got to Do with It?

Ultimately, the twin phenomena of Bloom's book on Shakespeare and the Oprah Book Club draw attention to a key
topic in this question of professional amateurs and amateur
professionals: the old, and new, question of love that is crucial to the field of literary criticism. I want, therefore, to close
by briefly taking note of a suggestive shift of emphasis within
the humanities that bears directly on the matters we have
been discussing: the so-called "return to aesthetics" and connoisseurship.

There has been much heralding of the return to aesthetics
lately, accompanied by pull-quotes that make it seem more
endangered and endangering than it is. Aesthetics is "the forbidden subject," "the bad child no one wants to talk about,"
two scholars told the *Chronicle of Higher Education*.[67] This may
once have been the case; there was a time not too long ago
when the mark of the professional literary scholar was an engagement with history or politics or the sociology of literature rather than with what, in a yet older tradition, was called
"appreciation." Resistance to the discussion of aesthetic plea-

sure in the classroom seems to have been premised in part on the idea that such pleasure bordered on "connoisseurship," an ideal of the amateur elite. And if scholars could disagree about the aesthetic quality of a work of art without one of them being right and the other wrong, if value was plural and descriptions of beauty or pleasure could be contradictory, what then was the authority of the critic, or of the work of art?

On the one hand aesthetic appreciation was too easy, and on the other hand it was too hard. In any event, no matter how personally moved by an art object or a literary passage the critic might be, he or she had considerable professional incentive for setting aesthetic judgment aside in favor of social, historical, or cultural analysis. But the "forbidden subject" is now on everyone's lips, and the "bad child" is—surprise!—the prodigal returned. Almost everyone wants to talk about it: a concern with aesthetics and ethics, the reappearance of certain notions of "value" and "values" on the literary scene, has preempted the stage, moving critical attention away from a previous decade's concerns with politics and cultural identity. It is worth noting that this quite natural—and, indeed, again, inevitable—turn of the wheel, which has been repeated in every literary-scholarly generation (remember the move from the Old Philology to New Criticism?) is closely connected to the "love" question that always hovers so closely (like a pesky putto) around both "amateur" and "literature."

When emeritus English professor Wayne Booth, the author of important books on rhetoric and fiction, writes one on "the glories of amateurism" called *For the Love of It*, extolling in terms a reviewer called "unembarrassed" and "effu-sive" the pleasure of playing chamber music with friends, Booth's authority as a literary scholar is what gives cre-dence—and piquancy—to his amatory confessions.[68] "For more than 40 years he has been regularly practicing the cello, creating unusual counterpoint to his work as a teacher of rhetoric, irony, and fictional narrative," wrote music critic and book reviewer Edward Rothstein. Rhetoric, irony, and fiction are here offered, unemphatically but unmistakably, as elements situated at the other end of the scale from the pas-sion and lost "idyllic" romanticism of "the amateur spirit," exemplified by the "grown men weeping at Haydn and sober scholars sobbing with Beethoven" that are lovingly chroni-cled in Booth's book.[69] (This is not Booth's own view, neces-sarily; his "heroes" are professionals who play with amateurs for pleasure. "Pro-amateurs," he calls them.)

Amateur status has, indeed, become almost de rigueur as a claim for some practicing literary professionals. Author, critic, and editor Wendy Lesser published an engaging book of essays called *The Amateur* in which she declared herself to be an "eighteenth-century man of letters, though one who happens to be female and lives in twentieth-century Berke-ley."[70] To her, amateurism meant the possibility of hanging out in coffeehouses and theaters, and refusing "to have arbi-trary lines drawn between things: between old masterpieces and contemporary works, between art and the rest of the world, between criticism and conversation." What's fascinat-ing here is that this is a perfect description of what some scholars within the university call cultural studies, a wide-ranging intellectual curiosity that has, from the time of Mon-

taigne, always characterized the speculative essay. Yet the arbi-
trary line Lesser so rightly wishes to avoid drawing between
categories in the liberal arts is one she is still willing to draw
in terms of the amateur and the professional, deciding (in
the admiring phrase of one reviewer) to "steer clear of the
academic profession" in order "to pursue what she loves."[71]
Is the longtime editor of the *Threepenny Review* really an amateur? Or is the word *amateur* the best tactical way of describing, and insulating, a certain kind of speculative writing—a
kind of writing that Lesser does not principally associate with
professional scholarship? As she would surely acknowledge,
this kind of writing has been long favored by, and is again
newly popular among, some of the most widely read and respected members of the academic profession.

"Criticism," wrote R. P. Blackmur in 1935, "is, I take it, the
formal discourse of an amateur."[72] The self-deprecating quali-
fier, "I take it," is itself a genial gesture in the direction of
amateurism. Blackmur's own "amateur" status was certified
by his training, or rather his lack of it. He had no formal
education after high school, yet became a professor of English at Princeton and a key theorist of the New Criticism.
We might compare him to other distinguished scholars and
teachers, such as Harry Levin, who was a Junior Fellow at
Harvard and had no Ph.D. The *absence* of the degree was in
this case a sign of high status.[73]

Hazard Adams describes Blackmur's dictum ("Criticism is, I
take it, the formal discourse of an amateur") as a "well-known
ironic phrase" and glosses it away: "he does not mean that
the critic should be a dilettante, but that he should be the

opposite of a 'professional' insofar as he is not 'professing' a doctrine."[74] But Blackmur's famous phrase is the opening salvo of an essay with a title that is perhaps equally ironic: "The Critic's Job of Work." The "well-known ironic phrase" about the critic as amateur is a knowing gesture of disavowal, a statement in fact about the profession and the professional responsibility of the critic. The job of the critic is to account for love.

Put very briefly, what the return to aesthetics and connoisseurship does is to situate the professional/amateur conundrum *within* professional academic discourse, making "love" the subject and object of study. By making appreciation—love, delight, affection, virtuosity—part of the mission of academia, such a move adroitly preempts the outsider's critique that today's humanities scholars have abandoned "appreciation" for microanalysis. The terms that are developed in Kant's *Critique of Judgment* to account for the analysis of beauty—disinterestedness, universality, something valued in itself and not for any "end," the production of "necessary delight"[75]—become precisely the qualities of the amateur as over against the professional. And yet these amateurs are professionals.

Nowadays amateurism seems to be the goal of the profession. But it turns out that the professional makes the best amateur.

And this, too, is a virtuoso move.

2

DISCIPLINE ENVY

I would I had bestowed that time in the tongues
that I have in fencing, dancing, and bear-baiting.
O, had I but followed the arts!
—Sir Andrew Aguecheek, *Twelfth Night*

CONFLICTS among the academic disciplines are often compared to turf battles and boundary disputes, likely to inspire
the planting of "Keep Off the Grass" signs and cries of "Not in
my back yard!" But let's not forget that other familiar proverb
about turf: "The grass is always greener in someone else's
yard."[1] This Aesop-like saying describes a common illusion
and a common mechanism of desire. It's not completely an
accident, I think, that the aphorism contains both turf
("yard") and greenness—the color of envy. What I want to
suggest is that disciplinary turf battles themselves both inspire, and depend upon, such trespassing.

There's a nice term that architectural planners use to describe the footpaths worn in the turf from one building or
paved pathway to another, the shortcuts chosen by pedestri-
ans and marked by their frequent traffic. The planners call
them "desire lines." Often, when they are well worn, these

"lines" in the grass will themselves be paved over, trans-
forming them from renegade or "scofflaw" passages into new,
officially sanctioned routes. In this fashion members of the
public, the users of buildings and structures, reconstitute
the space that links and separates institutions and autho-
rized channels. "Desire lines" are a feature of many public
walking spaces, but they are especially noticeable on college
campuses.

It is interesting to recall that the medieval divisions of
knowledge, the trivium and quadrivium, take their names
from the Latin terms for the place where three, and then
four, roads meet. (The trivium, the basic building blocks of
education, consisted of grammar, logic, and rhetoric; the
quadrivium, the next stage of learning, comprised geometry,
astronomy, arithmetic, and music.)

Boundary marking by disciplines, demarcating what does
and doesn't count as history or philosophy or literary studies,
is about training and certification and belonging to a guild,
but it is also, sometimes, about "the narcissism of minor differences"—a sibling rivalry among the disciplines.

Minor Differences

Freud's argument about the narcissism of small differences
appears in his discussion of group psychology, where he ex-
trapolates from a perception about individuals to a perception about groups: "almost every intimate emotional relation
between two people which lasts for some time—marriage,
friendship, the relations between parents and children—

contains a sediment of feelings of aversion and hostility." The same thing happens with groups, he says, and there the hostility is less cloaked by repression: "of two neighboring towns each is the other's most jealous rival; every little canton looks down upon the others with contempt. Closely related races keep each other at arm's length; the South German cannot endure the North German, the Englishman casts every kind of aspersion upon the Scot, the Spaniard despises the Portuguese."[2]

Similarity and contiguity, says Freud, breed distrust, rivalry, comparison, even, perhaps, self-hatred or self-doubt projected upon the nearby other. Each group is saying to itself, in effect, "I am not like that. If you look closely, you can see." What appears to be a family resemblance needs to be disavowed as part of the project of constituting the self.

Disciplines have, historically, often founded themselves on such "minor differences." Take the case of philosophy. In the works of Plato, philosophy is founded on its distinction from sophistry. Yet sophistry continually comes back to haunt philosophy.

The word *sophist* comes from a Greek word meaning "wise," "clever," or "expert," and the modern ambivalence about these categories can tell us something about the problem. A "sophistry" today is a piece of fallacious, if plausible, argument; the word is also parent to our concept of "sophistication," which has only recently come to mean "Cole Porter–cool"; its older sense included falsification, disingenuous alteration or perversion, and the corruption of a literary text in the course of copying or printing, as well as worldly wisdom, subtlety, discrimination, and expertise.

In a syllabus for a course on "History of Education" in 1907, John Dewey described the sophists as "a class of professional teachers," the first such class in the history of Europe. Dewey saw them as teachers of rhetoric (aiming "to train effective speakers and writers") and of political science (calling "attention to the training of the arts relating to statesmanship").[3] The British pragmatist F.C.S. Schiller, writing in the same year, described them as "university extension lecturers hampered by no university."[4] They offered, for a fee, instruction in public speaking for young men of the upper classes who aspired to political influence in an increasingly democratic Athens. An entry in *The Oxford Classical Dictionary* compares them to "the numerous institutions at the present day which advertise their ability to train people for success in business, or in life in general."[5]

Professional teachers? Humanists? Professional skeptics? The Dale Carnegies of Attic life? The sophists, who lost the battle of history, get no respect. They are just itinerant educators, out to make a buck (or a drachma), not genuine intellectuals in pursuit of "truth." But philosophy depends upon them, in more ways than than one. Here is Jacques Derrida's analysis, from his essay "Plato's Pharmacy":

> The front line that is violently inscribed between Platonism and its closest other, in the form of sophistics, is far from being unified, as if stretched between two homogeneous areas. Its design is such that, through a systematic indecision, the parties and the party lines frequently exchange their respective places, imitating the forms and borrowing the paths of the opponent.

Sophistics is the evil twin, the "closest other," that enables philosophy to define itself *as* philosophy precisely because it is not sophistics. But philosophy *is* sophistics, in that it appropriates some arguments (sophistically?) from sophistics in order to marshal them against the sophists. Thus, for example, Kierkegaard in *The Concept of Irony* argues that Socrates *must* use sophistry against the sophists, because if you live in "untruth" you cannot be attracted to the truth by the truth.[6] This argument from purity and expulsion is one that is all too familiar in political life, but also, mutatis mutandis, in intellectual—or rather, disciplinary—life. If, at the beginning of any discipline's self-definition, it undertakes to distinguish itself from another, "false" version of itself, that difference is always going to come back to haunt it.

A Seat at the Table

Differentiation is one strategy that disciplines employ to protect themselves against incursion and self-doubt. But how about the opposite strategy: emulation, imitation, envy? Here is what might be taken as an uncannily prescient snapshot of contemporary academic life, taken from the works of one of the great disciplinary trespassers of the last century, a mathematician, photographer, church deacon, and sometime fiction writer.

There was a table set out under a tree in front of the house, and the March Hare and the Hatter were having tea at it: a Dormouse was sitting between them, fast asleep, and the

other two were using it as a cushion, resting their elbows on
it, and talking over its head. . . .

The table was a large one, but the three were all crowded
together at one corner of it. "No room! No room!" they cried
out when they saw Alice coming. "There's *plenty* of room!"
said Alice indignantly, and she sat down in a large arm-chair
at one end of the table.

"Have some wine," the March Hare said in an encouraging
tone.

Alice looked all round the table, but there was nothing on
it but tea. "I don't see any wine," she remarked.

"There isn't any," said the March Hare.

"Then it wasn't very civil of you to offer it," said Alice
angrily.

"It wasn't very civil of you to sit down without being in-
vited," said the March Hare.

"I didn't know it was *your* table," said Alice: "it's laid for a
great many more than three." . . .

"I want a clean cup," interrupted the Hatter: "let's all move
one place on."

He moved as he spoke, and the Dormouse followed him:
the March Hare moved into the Dormouse's place, and Alice
rather unwillingly took the place of the March Hare. The Hatter was the only one who got any advantage from the change:
and Alice was a good deal worse off than before, as the March
Hare had just upset the milk-jug into his plate.[7]

Let this little vignette stand, for a moment, as a kind of paradigm or parable for what I will be calling "discipline envy." I
will leave it to you to cast the parts and decide whether Hat-

ter, March Hare, Dormouse, and Alice might usefully be equated to (just for example) philosophy, English, history, and cultural studies.

Everyone wants a seat at the table. But whose table *is* it? And is the progress from seat to seat among the disciplines (and interdisciplines) more like the Mad Hatter's tea party, where there are more than enough places for everyone, or, say, a game of musical chairs, in which each time the music stops there is one *less* seat for the players to occupy?[8]

The figure of "musical chairs" has a disconcerting literality in academic life, where distinguished "endowed chairs" often themselves cross the boundaries of the disciplines. What is the proper disciplinary home for a chair in "Aesthetics and the Theory of Value," or "Social Ethics," or "Law and Psychiatry in Society"—all endowed chairs at major universities? It will tell you something about the Mad Hatter aspect of scholarly classification that the last-named chair, "Law and Psychiatry in Society," is held by a professor of English and comparative literature.

Perhaps I should say something here about the word *envy* and the sense in which I'm using it. I want to emphasize that the system I am describing here is not one of envious persons but of disciplinary envy.

I can anticipate that praising or valorizing envy might be a hard sell, especially as linked with the world of scholarship. But I use *envy* here to designate a mechanism, a kind of energy, an exhilarating intellectual curiosity, as well as what Veblen called emulation.[9] Envy in this sense is not the same as jealousy ("fear of losing some good through the rivalry of another; resentment or ill-will toward another on account of advantage or superiority"). Rather it corresponds to older notions of the word that are generally positive rather than negative: a "desire to equal another in achievement or excellence; emulation" and (a sense derived from the French *envie*) a "wish, desire, longing; enthusiasm."[10]

Envy was a concept central to Greek culture, both intellectually and militarily. It underwrote the concept of competition, *agon,* which led to greatness. It's a word that can still scandalize us, as René Girard notes in his study of Shakespeare, calling envy "the provocative word, the astringent and unpopular word," closely linked to both emulation and desire.[11] As a friend said to me, urging me not to disavow the concept of envy, "It seems to me that envy might be that which makes intellectual life exciting, both to amateurs and to professionals."

My own upbringing did not involve a training in the "seven deadly sins," but it seems to me as a lay observer that all of these "sins" are in a way virtues taken to excess, and that they are to a certain extent (again I speak here nontheologically) recuperable by turning their energy toward what psychoanalysis might call a "good object." "Discipline envy" is, when practiced by scholars, also "disciplined envy," aspiration submitted to a regimen of authority and control.

In insisting on the word *envy* with all its history and the ambivalence that naturally attaches to it, I take some comfort from the example of zoologist Richard Dawkins, who encountered a similar resistance, and a similar misunderstanding, in relation to the word *selfish*. His best-selling book *The Selfish Gene* carefully explained that he was not *advocating* selfishness but *describing* it. "I am not advocating a morality based on evolution," he wrote. "I am saying how things have evolved." Yet, predictably, Dawkins was attacked for supposedly maintaining the very moral position he was at careful pains to disavow. As he reported in the second edition, "Critics have occasionally misunderstood *The Selfish Gene* to be advocating selfishness as a principle by which we should live!"[12]

As with selfishness, so with envy.

To repeat, then: It's not a matter of envious *individuals* (academic life has its share of these, but probably no more or less than any other profession) but of an intellectual inquiry that "envies," that desires. That is structured as a desire.

Coveting Your Neighbor's Discipline

Let me come directly, then, to the phenomenon of my title, "Discipline Envy."

This will be a familiar concept, even without any glossing. It's the wish, on the part of an academic discipline, to model itself on, or borrow from, or appropriate the terms and vocabulary and authority figures of another discipline. We might say the wish is on the part of "some members of" an academic discipline. But in fact anthropomorphism has its uses. And for me "discipline envy," which is very much a fact of life in my own academic discipline, literary studies, is a kind of fantasizing of an "ego ideal" elsewhere. In history, say, or philosophy, just to cite two of the most recent and powerful fantasmatic models for literary study.

But discipline envy, of course, is really a very old story.

In a treatise variously called a *Defence of Poesie* or an *Apologie for Poetrie*, written in 1580 and published in 1595, Sir Philip Sidney produced an excellent and witty account of "discipline envy" *avant la lettre*, when he compares poets to astronomers, mathematicians, and especially to their chief rivals, philosophers and historians. The *Defence of Poesie* was itself, significantly, a response to a diatribe against poetry and imaginative writing by a Puritan critic.

Moral philosophers, says Sidney, are often pedants and hypocrites, "sophistically speaking against subtlety." Philosophers are "obscure and deliberately difficult," historians "obsessed with old mouse-eaten records." The historian criticizes the philosopher for being abstract and prides himself on providing real archival data. But the poet is better than both the philosopher and the historian, says Sidney, because poetry is precept and example at once.[13] It was poetry that the other arts ought to envy. At least, according to the poet and diplomat Philip Sidney.

Here is another historical example of discipline envy:

A hundred years ago it was without question *music* that was the discipline of disciplines, the ideal, the ego ideal for the arts. Schelling and Goethe both compared architecture to "frozen music," and the power of this comparison had gained force by the end of the nineteenth century.[14] "All art constantly aspires toward the condition of music," wrote Walter Pater, famously. This is Pater's account of discipline envy:

> Although each art has . . . its own specific order of impressions, and an untranslatable charm . . . it is noticeable that, in its special mode of handling its given material, each art may be observed to pass into the condition of some other art, by what German critics term an *Anders-streben*—a partial alienation from its own limitations, through which the arts are able, not indeed to supply the place of each other, but reciprocally to lend each other new forces.

Pater notes the striving of some pieces of music toward "figure" and "pictorial definition," of architecture toward painting or poetry or sculpture, of sculpture toward color, of French poetry toward the art of engraving. But he reserves his most definitive statement for the idealization of music:

> All the arts in common aspir[e] toward the principle of music;
> music being the typical, or ideally consummate art, the object
> of the great *Anders-streben* of all art, of all that is artistic, or
> partakes of artistic qualities. *All art constantly aspires toward the*
> *condition of music.*[15]

Other writers and critics in this period agreed. Oscar Wilde
praised Pater's view of "music as the type of all the arts."[16] For
Stéphane Mallarmé music was ultimately a metaphor for the
structure of what he called "the totality of universal relation-
ships." Yeats's poetry—strongly influenced, at least in its early
years, by the aestheticism of Pater and Wilde—rhapsodized
about the "body swayed to music," and asked, rhetorically,
"How can we tell the dancer from the dance?" The answer,
of course, was that in good poetry, as in the other arts, we
couldn't and shouldn't.

It's not surprising to find that these figures—Wilde, Pater,
Yeats, Mallarmé—are as famous for their criticism as for their
literary accomplishments; in fact, for some of them the two
achievements are the same. The fusion that they have
achieved—this perfect synchrony of the intellectual and the
aesthetic—is in fact, we might say, *enabled* by the fantasy (however right or wrong) that such a fusion was already present
in another art form. In music.

Now we might pause to notice that Pater did *not* say, "All
art aspires to the condition of *musicology*," or even "All criticism or theory of art aspires to the condition of musicology."
He is talking about music, and he is talking about it in a very
abstract, idealized way. In fact, this *fantasy* of "music," if I can
put it that way, is probably unrecognizable to musicologists

as having anything to do with music at all, much less with musicology. These idealizations, seductive and unitary, are often produced and tended from outside a discipline rather than from within it. Sometimes the people who have the most definitive ideas about what is and is not "poetry" or "literature" are self-declared amateurs rather than professionals or professors. But none of this is to deny the sheer rhetorical and seductive power of Pater's formulation, or the importance of this kind of "aspiration" of one art or discipline toward another. It is, in fact, very recognizable as a *structure of desire*.

Is there a modern hierarchy of the disciplines? Toward what condition do today's disciplines aspire? In answer to the question "Which field of science has the smartest people?" (posed by "the only humor magazine with eight Nobel Prize laureates on its board"),[17] an astronomer offered the following response:

> Speaking of ranking the various disciplines—
> Politicians think they are Economists.
> Economists think they are Social Scientists.
> Social Scientists think they are Psychologists.
> Psychologists think they are Biologists.
> Biologists think they are Organic Chemists.
> Organic Chemists think they are Physical Chemists.
> Physical Chemists think they are Physicists.
> Physicists think they are Mathematicians.
> Mathematicians think they are God.
> God . . . ummm . . . so happens that God is an Astronomer.[18]

Over this past century alone my own discipline of literary studies has yearned to be, or to model itself on: linguistics, anthropology and ethnography; social science, natural science, psychoanalysis, sociology, history, and various strands of philosophy, from aesthetics to ethics.

Yet literary study has sometimes been itself the object of emulation. A decade or so ago historians, or at least some of them, were talking about "the linguistic turn," history's attraction to poststructuralist theory; or "the cultural turn," history's attraction to cultural anthropology. (More recently they've been writing books and articles like *Beyond the Cultural Turn* and "Is All the World a Text?"[19]) Art history today deploys methods and terminology that were formative for literary studies, like semiotics, psychoanalysis, and new historicism. In theater and dance studies, the disciplines that are most envied and copied are anthropology, history, and gender theory.

"Dry" sciences over "wet" sciences, quantitative social sciences over qualitative social sciences, "rational choice" over social and psychological determination, numbers over narration, philosophy over literary criticism and theory, literary theory over literary criticism, theorists in general over practitioners. In departments of psychology the neuroscientists reign, while proponents of "social" and "developmental" psychology may be regarded as "soft." Sigmund Freud, of course, is nowhere to be found in any department of psychology these days, just as Marx is viewed as irrelevant (or worse) in departments of economics and, indeed, of politics. However, along with Hegel and Kant, Marx and Freud are treated as major authors in departments of literature.

Virtually everyone in the humanities envies the philosophers, but the philosophers, some of them at least, aspire to the condition of law. Or, alternatively, to the condition of cognitive science.

Like envy itself, "discipline envy" is a mechanism—a structure. And it's the structure, not the hierarchy of the disciplines, that endures. The prestige and power of individual disciplines vary over time. New disciplines develop; others fade away. Envy, or desire, or emulation, the fantasy of becoming that more complete other thing, is what repeats.

I think we need to take cognizance of this tendency in academic and intellectual life to imagine that the truth, or the most revealing methods, or the paradigm with the answer, is just over the road apiece—in your neighbor's yard or department or academic journals rather than your own.

Sometimes fantasies like these are acknowledged (the anthropologist decides to use semiotics, the historian spends a year in medical school, the literary scholar studies law). At other times they are not. In the latter case the claim is made that the desired methods and paradigms were always to be found at home, in the original discipline. This is what often underlies the call to keep the disciplines "pure." If I am right in suggesting that "contamination" is already there, then "purity" is always another name for another impurity.

The *envy* tag has been popular, and indeed well-nigh ubiquitous, since the translation of Freud's word *penisneid* as "penis envy" in the standard edition of his works. "The psychical consequences of envy for the penis," he says, "are various and far reaching" and "quickly extend both to jealousy and to self-doubt and self-contempt." In the wake of Freud's claim that little girls suffer a narcissistic wound when they realize their own physical inferiority, and that adult women begin to share the contempt felt by men for their sex, there was, inevitably, a reaction. Bruno Bettelheim drew attention to womb or vagina envy in males, Melanie Klein noted that the maternal breast was the first object of envy for both boys and girls,[20] and later writers, like Irene Fast, suggested that the problem for *both* sexes was one of encountering limits within gendered identity.[21]

In the tendency to gender the disciplines we see an echo of this structure. In the middle and late twentieth century, the sciences and the quantitative social sciences have sometimes been stereotypically regarded as "masculine," serious, and hard. The opposite of *hard*, in this context, is not *easy* but *soft*, as in the common academic phrase, "the soft social sciences"—meaning those that use narrative, interpretive, and descriptive techniques rather than crunching numbers. An article in *Lingua Franca* details the claim by feminist economists that "the economics profession has been smothered by unmitigated masculinity," that its emphasis on rational choice theory and "math-for-math's sake" has made it "a boys' game in the sandbox."

I do not intend to elaborate further here on this particular idea of Freud's as it affects our understanding of maleness, femaleness, and sexual desire—few scholars these days, feminist or unfeminist, academic or lay, want to spend a lot of time on "penis envy"—but I do want to take a moment to discuss its usefulness as a model. For like so many of Freud's ideas, this one offers a good *model for thinking*, rather than a direct, unproblematic intuition about bodies and genders.

Here is what I take Freud and his followers to be saying. A belief develops in a class of persons, based on perceived (or conceived) inferiority: another class of persons, already more socially or politically powerful and more highly esteemed, is thought to possess the real thing, of which one's own version is "inferior," smaller, bogus, merely titillating, insignificant. That this is the structure of thinking that dominates much of academic life, both within and among the disciplines and divisions and between so-called "academia" and "real life," will not strike many as astonishing.

In current psychological shorthand, *envy* means not having it all: feeling a sense of loss, or limit, or even—I want to suggest—nostalgia for a past imagined as more perfect and more whole. For Melanie Klein, envy is an aspect of idealization, idealization gone wrong: "the subject envies the object for some possession or quality"[22] and "the more ideal the object, the more intense the envy."[23] "Envy," writes Jessica Benjamin, "is often a signal of thwarted identification."[24] Envy, indeed, may *be* thwarted identification, which is one reason why it is so often linked to that most unappealing and besetting "sin" of professional life, *Schadenfreude*, "malicious glee," pleasure at the suffering of others.

"Envy is concealed admiration," says Søren Kierkegaard. When an admirer "senses that devotion cannot make him happy," he changes his tune: "he will speak a different language, and in this language he will now declare that that which he really admires is a thing of no consequence, something foolish, illusory, perverse and high-flown."[25]

The *envy* tag itself pops up everywhere in contemporary culture. "We have developed a bad case of magnitude envy," wrote *New York Times* columnist Maureen Dowd. "In a culture obsessed with entertainment, celebrity, buzz, spin, market share, synergy, gestures, decaf skim latte and cigar bars, we feel diminished and puny. We have developed a craving for real nobility, large principles, passions with scale and profound commitments."[26] (The topic of Dowd's essay, symptomatically enough, was treason, which she found more major and principled in the time of Hiss and the Rosenbergs than in the diminished era of Linda Tripp. Even treason was better in the old days.)

In her book *The Feminization of American Culture*, historian Ann Douglas made clever use of the term, describing the "pulpit envy" that overcame many women in the northern United States during the nineteenth century. Women admired their ministers, wrote biographies of them by the thousands, and ultimately wished to be them. "If the minister was like a woman," with a tender and gentle heart, "why shouldn't the woman be like a minister" and preach powerfully in church?[27]

There are currently not two but three books that go under the title *Venus Envy*; one is a history of cosmetic surgery, another a polemical essay about fatherhood in contemporary fiction, and the third a lesbian novel by Rita Mae Brown.[28] A literary-critical study of gay writers as amateur keyboard musicians begins with a section called "Pianist Envy."[29]

And—my personal favorite among the *envy* coinages—a wine store near my house put a big sign in its window announcing (or inviting) what it called "Pinot Envy."

But *envy* as a tag has also been applied, quite specifically, to disciplinary—and literary—desires. An article in the *New York Times* "Week in Review" section about the spate of books

written (or ghostwritten) by TV anchors, called the phenomenon a symptom of a "classic sense of pencil envy."[30]

Now, few writers today really work in pencil, I would guess,
though editors do. The word processor carries all before it.
But "pencil envy" not only offers a nice near-homology to
"penis envy" but also gestures nostalgically toward the lost
"real" of writing for *writers*, when everything was done, sans
Spell Check and Lexis-Nexis, painstakingly by hand.

Journalist to author may be one axis of envy, though it's
clearly one fraught with ambivalence. (Would any of these
anchorpersons really want to be researchers? Professors?
With professors' salaries?) But another axis, one located
within, rather than on the fringes of, what cultural observers
like to call "the academy," is that of humanist to scientist or
social scientist to natural scientist. Psychologist and educator
Howard Gardner writes that "During its period of 'physics
envy,' psychology attempted as much as possible to ape the
methods of physical science, setting up pure laboratory conditions and removing from the experiment any vestiges of
familiarity or context." And, reporting on the ease with which
physicist Alan Sokal's hoax paper was accepted by the editors
of *Social Text*, another *Times* reporter diagnosed it as a case of
"science envy."[31] Science has "such prestige and power,"
wrote journalist Edward Rothstein, because "in science there
exist facts and truths that are invariant—unaltered by culture, politics, and prejudices."[32] He accused *Social Text*'s
editors and defenders—prominent among them, Stanley
Fish—of "gazing at science's privileged position with envy
and condescension."

The accusation of science envy, with or without that catchy phrase, is writ large in Sokal and Bricmont's critique of what they call "postmodern intellectuals' abuse of science." The claim of envy first surfaces in the introduction, when the authors offer some "psychological" guesswork about the motives of writers like psychoanalyst Jacques Lacan and historian Bruno Latour. "They imagine, perhaps, that they can exploit the prestige of the natural sciences in order to give their own discourse a veneer of rigor."[33]

Imagining Interdisciplinarity

One response to envy is to try to have it all, which in disciplinary terms means interdisciplinarity.

"*Interdisciplinary* studies, of which we hear so much," writes one of my favorite critics, "do not merely confront already constituted disciplines (none of which, as a matter of fact, consents to *leave off*). In order to do interdisciplinary work, it is not enough to take a 'subject' (a theme) and to arrange two or three sciences around it. Interdisciplinary study consists in creating a new object, which belongs to no one."[34] The critic was Roland Barthes. The year was 1972—almost thirty years ago.

We still hear much, perhaps too much, about interdisciplinary studies: their desirability, their impossibility, their inevitability, their courtship of imposture.

In an essay in the MLA journal *Profession*, Stanley Fish claimed that when people say they are doing interdisciplinary studies, they are either (1) borrowing information or techniques from other disciplines to execute their own disciplinary tasks or (2) working within a discipline at a time when it is expanding its own boundaries and methodologies, as English departments were thought to do in the 1980s, or (3) establishing a new discipline, "one that takes as its task the analysis of disciplines," and thus besting the enterprise while at the same time calling it into question.[35] By the terms of this analysis, interdisciplinary studies are not merely, as Fish's suggests, "very hard to do"; they are impossible, since they disappear, like a reflection in water, whenever they are touched. Alternatively, we are always already interdisciplinary.

Many people have taken a skeptical view of such interdisciplinary work in the humanities.

When she was president of the Modern Language Association in 1980, literary critic Helen Vendler spoke out forcefully against what she called "a general interdisciplinary Polonius-like religious-historical-philosophical-cultural overview."[36] Vendler urged her hearers to maintain "our own separateness from other disciplines." More recently, in his own term as president, Edward Said voiced some of the same concern for wholeness, or what he called "intellectual coherence," in a column in the *MLA Newsletter*. "All manner of fragmented, jargonized subjects of discussion now flourish in an ahistorical limbo. They are not completely anthropological or sociological or philosophical or psychological, although they seem to carry some of the marks of all those disciplines."[37] Both of these scholars, and many others, have been wary of crossover work that seems too facile, not well grounded or well researched, work that seems merely to borrow the "marks" or terminology or moves of a discipline rather than its underlying habits of thought. In particular, such critiques point toward the necessary integrity of disciplinary training, the fact that you can't be "interdisciplinary" until you are "disciplinary," or well disciplined, in at least one traditional field of study.

I don't disagree with these judgments or this prudent caution, though I am perhaps somewhat less alarmed by recent interdisciplinary developments, which I see in part as intellectual and institutional growing pains. Clearly there is good and less good interdisciplinary work, just as there is good and less good work within a discipline. Exciting and convincing interdisciplinary work stages a really intensive encounter of two or more disciplines, with results that can be unexpected and disconcerting, but also path-breaking and sometimes brilliant. We might compare this kind of encounter to the pedagogical challenge of team teaching, often and quite wrongly thought of as easier than conventional teaching rather than more difficult. Two teachers in the classroom can flash ideas off one another in ways that are exhilarating for both of them, and for their students. But they also need to learn each other's mental moves, rhetoric, and styles of thought, taking nothing for granted. Otherwise both they and the students will be bothered and bewildered rather than bewitched. Nothing works better than team teaching, when it works; nothing falls flatter when it fails.

In fact, *interdisciplinary* is a word as much misunderstood these days as *multiculturalism*, and for similar reasons. Both words seem to their detractors to break down boundaries and hierarchies, to level differences rather than discriminate among them, to invite an absence of rigor, and to threaten—

somehow—to erase or destroy the root term (*culture, discipline*). It is as if new formations, like "science and literature" or "environmental studies" or "medical humanities" or "criminal justice" or "the new Jewish studies," to name just a random few of the "interdisciplines" in which students can now take courses and degrees, put in question the integrity and methods of science, literature, theology, philosophy, medicine, or law.[38]

Does interdisciplinarity trump the disciplines? Here's a practical example. I chaired a search committee, called "the Wild Card Committee," for my department. Our charge was to think of exciting scholars who didn't fit any traditional search category: people who worked in several fields or periods or who were cross- or interdisciplinary. Once the department accepted a recommendation from us, my job was to help the chairman redescribe the candidate as at the heart of a recognizable "field," a field which was on more than one occasion configured around the chosen scholar. He, or she, then "fit" the search description perfectly, of course. To my colleagues I reiterated the range of meanings that *wild* could carry, from untamed and undomesticated to enthusiastic and versatile. But if and when these scholars joined the department, they would become professors of English—not of Interdisciplinarity. The "discipline" would impose its own discipline upon them.

The impetus to cross or link the disciplines does not come only from scholars or authors; it also comes from publishers and bookstores. Have a look at the books on your shelf to see how the publisher wants them classified and shelved. On the back cover, usually on the top left corner, you'll find instructions. Pierre Bourdieu's book *On Television* is labeled "Sociology/Media Studies"; James Elkins's *The Poetics of Perspective* is "Art History/Aesthetics"; Foucault's *Discipline and Punish* is "Philosophy/Criminology"; my book *Dog Love* is "Psychology/Pets." It makes sense that the vendors should want more than one placement for their wares. The result, though, is a continuing sense of the restlessness or ambivalence of intellectual projects, their unwillingness to stay at home, where they belong.

In a testy op-ed piece on the trivialization of the Holocaust, Gabriel Schoenfeld, the senior editor of *Commentary*, took the opportunity to decry, in depressingly familiar terms, "the culture of victimhood, visible in our society at large but particularly ensconced in the universities." For Schoenfeld, the Holocaust, "the ultimate in victimization," was "simply assuming pride of place in a field that also comprises women's studies, gay and lesbian studies, disability studies, and all the other victim disciplines that today constitute the cutting edge of the academic world."[39]

Schoenfeld's position, when examined without the emotion that the particularity of the Holocaust so naturally produces, is fundamentally an anti-intellectual one. Some things are too important, too painful, too historic, too terrible, to be analyzed. Schoenfeld implicitly assigns the Holocaust to the realm of the *predisciplinary*. "Holocaust studies" as a discipline, the "academicization" (his jargon word, not mine) of the subject, is itself to be avoided.

So on the one hand there are things that are too important to become mere disciplines, like the Holocaust, and on the other hand there are things that are too *un*important to become disciplines, like gay and lesbian studies and disability studies.

Notice that the word *studies* here has become in a way a suspect piece of jargon. Yet it has had, until recently, a respectable history. In fact *studies* as a term has itself shifted over the last several decades from geographical regions and historical eras to cultural groups. It is perhaps most familiar from the concept of "area studies," where it identified a region (Latin American studies, South Asian studies, Middle Eastern studies) and a complex of scholarly interests and approaches. "Studies" were precisely *not* disciplines; they were interdisciplines, nexes of overlapping interest. As far as I can gather, this is a postwar (and a Cold War) coinage, a sign of the increasing interest in non-European or non-Western regions of the world. At the same time, of course, departments of and programs in "American studies" were appearing on the academic scene.[40]

We should add to this geographical notion of "studies" another, parallel development that was historical rather than specifically, or explicitly, regional: "medieval studies" and "Renaissance studies," for example. These "studies" were *temporal*, rather than *regional*. (Initially, the lack of a specified region indicated that they were primarily concerned with Western Europe.) In terms of academic prestige, both kinds of studies, after their initial "cutting edge" moment, were sometimes regarded as slightly "soft," because they were accretions rather than theoretical interventions. They did not shift paradigms but rather enshrined them. They were nothing if not respectable. But women's studies, Afro-American studies, and ethnic studies were something else. The very word *studies* had begun to take on a suspect "political" tinge, as if from the beginning "area studies"—founded on Cold War counterphobia—had not had intrinsic, and often manifest, political designs.

While the proliferation of "studies" in the humanities galls some commentators, few are exercised at the permutations of departments and programs in the natural sciences. I've seen no outrage at the founding of a Center for Genomics and Proteomics, nor any public outcry against such bastardizations as "biophysics," "neuroscience," or "environmental science and public policy," all relatively new entries in the course catalog.

Indeed, in the wake of "studies" that were anti- or cross- or interdisciplinary by design, the traditional disciplines have in some cases begun renaming themselves as "studies": English studies, literary studies, Romance studies. And these new "studies" include issues like culture, history, language, cartography, gender, and sexuality in the range of courses they offer. The cluster model more and more obtains, with or without the "studies" designation. To make a long story short, the once outside has become the new inside. Or, to take a longer historical view, that which was once considered collectively (in the grand old days of unified knowledge: the trivium and quadrivium) and was later individualized, categorized, classified, and assorted into "departments" is now again being viewed as a collectivity. With a difference. Whether we call this poaching, cultural imperialism, hegemony, interdisciplinarity, or the end of the intellectual world as we know it will depend upon where we're coming from, where we think we're going, and in what company.

It's worth noting that new disciplines, "interdisciplines," and paradisciplines are being formed all the time. We might think—and I advance this metaphor from science cautiously—of the useful notion of "deferents" and "epicycles" advanced by Ptolemy, the ancient astronomer. The problem for Ptolemy and his followers was that the heavenly bodies, supposed to move in orderly courses around the unmoving earth, failed to behave as predicted. So Ptolemaic astronomers tinkered with the cycles of the spheres, adding epicycles (smaller, corrective circles) in an effort to adjust the system rather than change it. Likewise with the still and unmoving disciplines: if they too are imagined as fixed, we will need more and more "studies" and "interdisciplines" to make them mirror the world.

Genius Envy

Ptolemy's mathematical ingenuity, of course, lasted only until the insights of Copernicus and others reimagined the solar system in another way. And the name Copernicus, or the term "Copernican revolution," suggests another way of understanding the phenomenon of what I have been calling "discipline envy." For by the terms of the analysis we have been pursuing, discipline envy is doomed to self-perpetuation. Tantalizingly just beyond reach is always another discipline to be conquered, another field or subfield to be mastered ("Clean cup, please"). The inevitable consequence of interdisciplinarity may not be the end of the scholarly world as we know it but the acknowledgment that our knowledge is always partial, rather than total. A difficult acknowledgment, for envy, as we have seen, wants it all.

So the "answer" to discipline envy is not the epicycle but Copernicus, the original thinker, the "genius." The powerful intellectual parent who will reimagine our world.

There's a certain irony here, because the Copernican revolution can be said to have *diminished* the egocentrism of mankind. But even when the "genius" takes away from us a belief or a paradigm we cherish, even when our own importance seems to be diminished, the genius himself stands tall. Copernicus; Darwin; and (love him or hate him) Freud. What I want to insist upon here is the importance of the "genius" to our cultural fantasy life. The longed-for totality, the bearer of authenticity, the "real thing," can be found in our love affair with the genius. For we do—make no mistake about it—have a crush on genius. And the concept of "genius," paradoxically, will help us to define the disciplines.

We ought to know what "genius" is. After all, we live in a time when so-called "genius grants" provided by the John D. and Catherine T. MacArthur Foundation identify, through what should be by now a familiar structure of back formation, the designated "geniuses" of our time. Although the foundation disavows the phrase "genius grants," the media love it.[41] In some ways the "genius grants" are like the Ph.D. program for public intellectuals mentioned in the first chapter. In each case institutional status virtually guarantees the *non*-achievement of the goal (becoming a public intellectual; becoming a genius), since a genius, whether domiciled in art or science, must almost by definition make or break rules, not follow them. To fit into the category (designated, grant-receiving "genius") is to be disciplined beyond the transcendent bounds of genius.

But what is a genius? And what does genius have to do with the disciplines?

The modern use of the term *genius* to denote self-generating brilliance, "native endowment," originality and creativity, is in fact a product of eighteenth-century thought.[42] Although this sense of the word seems to have originated in England, it came to its greatest prominence in Germany, where the "Sturm und Drang" period is also called the *Genieperiode*. The difference between genius and talent, like that between genius and learning, has to a certain extent shaped modern thinking about free-standing versus propped or dependent ability.

In a book significantly called *The Genius of Shakespeare*, Jonathan Bate suggests that " 'genius' was a category invented in order to account for what was peculiar about Shakespeare." As a playwright, Shakespeare broke all the rules: too many characters, too much gruesome detail, mingling kings and clowns. Why then were his plays such a success? He was a genius: indeed, *the* genius, the national poet, the source of patriotic pride and identification. Ben Jonson was far more "correct" and far more ostentatiously learned. Thus he was *not* a genius, merely a very fine dramatist.[43]

Increasingly in the eighteenth century, genius—poetic, artistic genius—was linked to being unlinked: unpropped, free-standing, unaccountable. In the *Spectator* papers Joseph Addison placed Shakespeare in the first order of geniuses, along with Homer, Pindar, and the Old Testament prophets, those "who by the mere Strength of natural Parts, and without any assistance of Art or Learning, have produced Works that were the Delight of their own Times, and the Wonder of Posterity."[44] By the time of Edward Young's *Conjectures on Original Composition* (1759), "originality" was being associated, not with going back to origins, but to freedom from them—the sense that it often has today.[45] Genius is *antithetical* to discipline.

If the "envy" of "discipline envy" is an envy of the idealized real, then it is also to a certain extent "genius envy," although one of the peculiar qualities of genius, that child of the Romantic period, is that by definition it attaches only to individuals, not to schools, methodologies, or disciplines. Shakespeare, Mozart, Leonardo da Vinci. Or as Kant, inevitably the oracle here, puts it,

> *Genius* is the talent (or natural gift) which gives the rule to art. Since talent, as the innate productive faculty of the artist, belongs itself to nature, we may express the matter thus: Genius is the innate mental disposition (*ingenium*) through which nature gives the rule to art.[46]

Genius is original; it steps off the beaten path, but inevitably to open up a new one which will be trodden, and paved, by disciples. What it produces must be "models, i.e., *exemplary*," capable of serving as a standard or rule of judgment for other (lesser) minds. It's important to note that for Kant the genius is, virtually by definition, a producer of art, not of (mere) science.[47]

Kant assures us that he means no slight to "those great men to whom the human race owes so much gratitude" for advancing and perfecting knowledge, but it is clear that for him art is of a different order from science: "it is quite ridiculous for a man to speak and decide like a genius in things which require the most careful investigation by reason."[48] And, yet again, "what is called *genius* . . . is a talent for art, not for science."[49]

For Kant, genius is in the province of the *humanities* and is not a product of reason but of inspiration. The genius is not a member of any school, though he (or, presumably, she, though this isn't a possibility that Kant envisages)[50] must provide models for imitation, the blueprint for a school or new methodology. Geniuses do not belong to disciplines. They may, however, influence, generate, or found them, despite themselves. We may say that they produce "disciples." Followers, adherents, pupils, believers, scholars, even "clones."

The genius, then, rightly considered, is the most envied object of "discipline envy," since the genius escapes the discipline of the disciplines. It is perhaps a significant measure of our distance from Kant that the term has migrated to a certain extent from art to science.

In a wonderfully lucid biography of physicist Richard Feynman entitled *Genius*, James Gleick traces the term's transition from tutelary spirit (*genius loci*, daemon, good or bad angel) to magician and wizard (Homer, Faustus, Copernicus, Michelangelo, Shakespeare, Mozart, Newton) to European Romantic madman (Baudelaire, Beethoven) to practical American inventor (Alexander Graham Bell, Samuel Morse, Eli Whitney, and above all "the wizard of Menlo Park," Thomas Alva Edison, who gave the world [electric] light).

"When otherwise sober scientists speak of the genius as magician, wizard, or superhuman," Gleick asks, "are they merely

indulging in a flight of literary fancy? When people speak of
the borderline between genius and madness, why is it so evi-
dent what they mean?" And why (a question that he says "has
barely been asked") has "the production of geniuses—Shake-
speares, Newtons, Mozarts, Einsteins—seemingly choked off
to nothing, genius itself coming to seem like the property of
the past?"[51]

The concept of a "genius" in the humanities did linger on,
as a kind of ghostly afterimage, in the early twentieth century,
especially as deployed by the circle around Gertrude Stein.
Here is Alice B. Toklas on the subject—or rather, Stein in the
voice of Toklas: "the geniuses came and talked to Gertrude
Stein, and the wives sat with me. . . . I have sat with wives who
were not wives, of geniuses who were real geniuses. I have sat
with real wives of geniuses who were not real geniuses. I have
sat with wives of geniuses, of near geniuses, of would be geniuses."[52] It is a little difficult to know where irony leaves off
here and genuine admiration begins, as the wives (and non-
wives) of figures like Picasso, Matisse, Hemingway, and
Braque make their appearances at the Rue de Fleurus. But it
is clear from this kind of litany, and from the title of Robert
McAlmon's contemporaneous memoir of the twenties, *Being
Geniuses Together*, that the word *genius* has faint quotation
marks around it: the term is a nostalgic survival, an endangered species.[53] (It is also clear that Gertrude Stein's chief
example of a modern genius was Gertrude Stein.)[54]

What I want to suggest is not only that the cultural identification of *genius* has in recent years come to focus on science
rather than on art but also that this very shift has created a
powerful nostalgia for the geniuses of yore. In a way we have

moved from the *genius* to the *gene*: We pretend, at least, that
we are looking for a gene for genius. But in a way the gene
has replaced the genius. The "answer" to Gleick's "barely
asked" question about the pastness of genius comes, I think,
from a kind of cultural *Schadenfreude*, a barely suppressed *desire* that there should be no more geniuses, as a way of certi-
fying the realness, the authenticity, the originality of the geniuses of the past.

Here is a nice fictional exploration of the limits and definitions of genius, as seen through the wry eyes of Virginia
Woolf. Her subject is the pretty-good philosopher Mr. Ram-
say, as he strides on his terrace and attempts "to arrive at
a perfectly clear understanding of the problem which now
engaged the energies of his splendid mind."

> [H]e could see, without wishing it, that old, that obvious
> distinction between the two classes of men; on the one hand
> the steady goers of superhuman strength who, plodding and
> persevering, repeat the whole alphabet in order, twenty-six
> letters in all, from start to finish; on the other the gifted, the
> inspired, who, miraculously, lump all the letters together in
> one flash—the way of genius. He had not genius; he laid no
> claim to that; but he had, or might have had, the power to
> repeat every letter of the alphabet from A to Z accurately in
> order. Meanwhile, he stuck at Q. On then, on to R.[55]

The philosopher's alphabetical progress marks him as no genius, merely a plodder of a very high order. And, as we will
see, the alphabet is often deployed as a sign of such dutiful
disciplinary perseverance.

But disciplinarity, even of the plodding type, has its own dark twin, in the specter of the *autodidact*. The autodidact is, by definition, not a member of "the discipline." As if to overcompensate for that fact, the autodidact is disciplined, even hyperdisciplined. He follows, almost compulsively, rules of his own making.

Consider Sartre's autodidact in *La Nausée* (or, as his English translator terms him, "the Self-Taught Man") reading the books in the library methodically from *A* to *Z*.

> One day, seven years ago . . . he came pompously into this reading-room. He scanned the innumerable books which lined the walls. . . . Then he went and took the first book from the first shelf on the far right; he opened to the first page, with a feeling of respect and fear mixed with an unshakeable decision. Today he has reached "L"—"K" after "J," "L" after "K." He has passed brutally from the study of coleopterae to the quantum theory, from a work on Tamerlaine to a Catholic pamphlet against Darwinism, he has never been disconcerted for an instant. He has read everything; he has stored up in his head most of what anyone knows about parthenogenesis, and half the arguments against vivisection. There is a universe behind and before him. And the day is approaching when closing the last book on the last shelf on the far left: he will say to himself, "Now what?"[56]

Or recall the duped pawnbroker of the Sherlock Holmes story "The Red-headed League," who spends his days in an office painstakingly copying out the Encyclopedia Britannica ("Eight weeks passed away like this, and I had written about Abbots and Archery and Armour and Architecture and

Attics, and hoped with diligence that I might get on to the B's before very long")[57] while thieves tunnel under his place of business. Or Flaubert's hapless clerks, Bouvard and Pécuchet. Or the Reverend Mr. Casaubon of George Eliot's *Middlemarch*, doggedly and self-importantly at work on his "Key to all Mythologies," a masterpiece of secondhand scholarship.[58]

In addition to these fictional autodidacts we might also include the titular madman of Simon Winchester's fascinating historical narrative *The Professor and the Madman*, Dr. William Chester Minor, a convicted murderer who supplied thousands of carefully culled quotations to the editor of *The Oxford English Dictionary* while confined to the asylum for criminal lunatics at Broadmoor.[59]

Why is the "discipline" of the autodidact so comical? What's *wrong* with reading books in alphabetical order by author, or indeed by color, or size, or Library of Congress call number? Why does Sartre describe his Self-Taught Man as an obsessional, never "disconcerted" (as presumably he should be) by the odd juxtapositions of his research?

The issue is one of authenticity and self-authentication. Dr. Minor, the madman, looked just like Professor James Murray, the lexicographer. As Winchester points out, the two men were "uncannily similar": both tall, thin, and bald, with deeply hooded blue eyes and strikingly similar long white beards. "Each man must have imagined, for a second, that he was stepping toward himself in a looking-glass, rather than meeting a stranger."[60] For many a scholar—though not, as it happens, for the equable Murray—this is the scholar's nightmare.

The autodidact is *not* a scholar, the scholar protests. He, or she, is not trained, makes elementary mistakes, thinks that knowledge can be collected, stored up.[61] The autodidact's industry puts the scholar and the intellectual into a quandary of self-questioning. If the self-taught man can mimic the scholar, the scholar sees his own vulnerability and his own fussy limits. And he reacts by disavowal.

The autodidact envies the scholar who inhabits a discipline. The scholar within the discipline sees the autodidact, as his uncanny double, from whom he must distinguish himself. Yet the whole nature of the discipline is, precisely, that it can't be self-taught. It must be transmitted ("given the rule," in Kant's phrase) in order to exist.

What Disciplines Envy

But what of our other term, *discipline*? Etymologically, it is distinguishable from *doctrine* (its narcissistic other) in that the doctrine belongs to the teacher and the discipline to the pupil, so historically, *doctrine* has been more concerned with abstract theory and *discipline* with practice or exercise. The idea of a "discipline" as a branch of knowledge or instruction goes back to medieval times, but the proliferation of "the disciplines" is a late-seventeenth- and eighteenth-century development. Indeed, a historian of philosophy could write in 1958: "It is only quite recently that the subject-matter, or rather the tasks, of philosophy have come to be clearly distinguished from those of other disciplines."[62] Suggestively, Foucault's *Discipline and Punish* aligns under one heading, "the means of correct training" that evolved in eighteenth-century Europe, such seemingly disconnected elements as the military camp, the scientific observatory, the elementary class-room, and the examination system, each of which has its structural counterpart in the modern university. Disciplines normalize, codify, collect, select; by means of documenta-tion, they make each individual a "case."

When "the disciplines" evolved, when "science" and "art" began (at least in a certain institutional way) to part company after the Renaissance, the very nature of narrative changed. The story that we tell ourselves about ourselves became not a story of exemplary "heroes" but a story of the typical, the normal, the ordinary, the calculated.

The birth of the disciplines was the death of the hero, Fou-cault implies, and (not coincidentally), the birth of psychol-ogy and psychoanalysis. "All the sciences, analyses, or prac-tices employing the root 'psycho-' have their origin in this historical reversal of the procedures of individualization."[63]

No wonder "the disciplines" have become gated communi-ties or combat zones. They are invitations to nostalgia, a long-ing for a lost unitary knowledge and a lost unitary self. And they have often turned that nostalgia inward, seeking a pure and wholer version of themselves.

So here is the paradox: the disciplines are constituted, pre-cisely, on the site of their own lack. They are, in fact, twice so constituted: First, because their desire is for genius, and ge-nius, as we have seen, does not follow given rules or tread familiar paths but rather, in Kant's phrase, gives the rule to a discipline. Second, because the disciplines are constituted by the asymptotic approach to an ideal of themselves. Their existence is bound up with the continual attempt to coincide with that ideal, and the equally continual, and equally inevitable, failure to do so. The space between the attempt and the idealization, the space of disciplinary desire, is what we call "theory." And this is why theory always, in a sense, fails; for when it succeeds, it ceases to be theory and becomes fact or doctrine. Then the desire, the desire line, moves elsewhere.

Disciplines envy themselves. That's why we can't—and indeed shouldn't wish to—find a "cure" for discipline envy. Envy is intrinsic to the very structure of disciplines. It is their indwelling spirit. It's what makes disciplines work. In the older sense of the term, envy is their *genius.*

An Academic Dream

In any discussion of "discipline envy" there will of course be unmentionable issues, some of which I want to be sure to mention. Some "academics" envy nonacademics: novelists, screenwriters, Washington insiders, activists, "public intellectuals"—anyone who seems to touch and to have influence upon the "real world."

But some "nonacademics" also envy academics. Journalists, CEOs, even public intellectuals if they are not actually "academics," have what is often called a love-hate relationship with the idea of professional scholarship. On the one hand, they sometimes think that professional scholars, like those low-prestige rhetoric teachers, the sophists, work for money and the enjoyment of their own cleverness, not for truth. On the other hand, partly because, for some people, schooldays are a nostalgia-filled memory, the idea that "academics" get to live in them full time (and get to be those most fantasized of power figures, *teachers*, who are arguably powerful *only* in dreams) produces ambivalence.

Remember that we were all students, once. Disciples, if you like. Professors are just the ones who stayed in school. Some people might say this is a sign of immaturity, or lack of imagination or guts. But others would say that we're the lucky ones. The ones who got to do this for a living. Becoming the teacher is one way of acting out "discipline envy." But it's also one way of reinstating it. Because inside almost every professor is someone who would really like to be a student again. This is another version of what I am calling nostalgia: the wish to be the lover, not the beloved; the questioner, not the person presumed to know. Interdisciplinarity feeds this desire, too: it allows the teacher to be a student once again.

The CEO or the journalist or the lawyer who likes to go to lectures at the Ninety-second Street Y, or to "alumni college," or to the local Shakespeare discussion group, probably cherishes a fantasy of academic life that academics only wish they could lead. A dream that the life of a scholar means spending most of one's time reading or talking about ideas, about poetry, about art. Alas, scholars dream of this too. As they go about the mundane but necessary "disciplinary" tasks of grading exams and attending committee meetings and holding office hours. This "life of the mind" is something we *all* envy. It is the *real*, if fantastical, Academy, the one with the capital *A*.

To address this point directly, and to close, let me briefly evoke a well-known pictorial image of this Academy, the great painting by Raphael known as *The School of Athens*. One of four murals in a room designed to hold Pope Julius II's personal library, *The School of Athens* depicts a gathering of the most famous philosophers of the ancient world. Raphael drew upon two familiar pictorial traditions, that of "Famous Men" (Uomini Famosi), or heroes of antiquity, and the Sacra Conversazione, the holy conversation.

The traditional Sacra Conversazione was a composition in which angels, saints, and sometimes donors occupied the same space as the Madonna and Child. It's a key trope in painting from the Renaissance onward (e.g., Fra Angelico in Florence and Bellini in Venice). Usually the figures are lost in meditation, however; Raphael transforms the trope by having them engaged in lively discourse. An assembly of philosophers are grouped around Plato and Aristotle, Plato clearly clutching a copy of his *Timaeus*, Aristotle his *Ethics*. The cynic Diogenes is on the steps; Zoroaster, whose back is turned, holds a globe of the heavens; geometers and astronomers are to the right, Pythagoras and his disciples to the left, identified by a slate with a musical diagram. Other clearly identified figures include Euclid, Ptolemy, Heraclitus, the Renaissance architect Bramante and the painter Raphael himself.[64]

What is especially relevant to my argument here is the magnificently *anachronistic* quality of the fresco, derived in part, as we've noted, from the Sacra Conversazione tradition, in which high-paying modern donors might see themselves depicted in (spiritual) conversation with Mary and the saints. Raphael secularizes this wishful fantasy and places himself in the picture, together with ancient Greeks, Ottoman Turks, his own mentor Donato Bramante, the architect of St. Peter's, and, perhaps, Raphael's contemporary Giovanni Bazzi, the painter known as "Il Sodoma."

In 1903, on the occasion of his seventieth birthday, the philosopher Wilhelm Dilthey delivered a lecture called "The Dream," in which he reported a scenario straight out of a medieval dream vision. He had spent the evening at a "friend's castle," where their philosophical conversation lasted deep into the night. Retiring to his "old familiar bedroom," he found himself facing an etching of Raphael's *School of Athens*. And when he slept, he dreamt that the figures of the philosophers came to life. Not only did they come to life, they divided into three camps: on the right of the picture the materialists or positivists, grouped around Archimedes and Ptolemy, who were joined by modern figures like Descartes and Leibniz; in the center stood Socrates and Plato, the idealists of freedom, joined by Kant, Schiller, Fichte, Carlyle, and ultimately by Descartes, who "separat[es] himself from the mathematical naturalists"; and on the left of the picture were Pythagoras and Heraclitus, the "objective idealists," including the moderns Schelling and Hegel ("walking hand in hand as in the days of their youth") and, surrounded by his fictional creations, Goethe. Dilthey was attracted at times to one group and at times to another; he "strove for the unity of thought" and, struggling, he awoke. His wish was to reconcile these differing perspectives. But in the dream he saw that each was both "true" and "one-sided."[65] He thought that he could intervene, that he himself could become part of Plato's Academy and resolve its disputes.

It would be scandalous to compare Raphael's incomparable masterpiece to popular modern film comedy, but let me just mention, in passing, the formal affinities this scenario has with Allen's *Zelig* (1983) or with *Forrest Gump* (1994), films in which our nondescript hero is inserted into old photographs and newsreel footage, thus appearing to be the contemporary of great events. Leonard Zelig too has his "sacred conversations," with public intellectuals like Susan Sontag, Saul Bellow, Irving Howe, and Bruno Bettelheim.

The School of Athens depicts a transcendent, multitemporal, interdisciplinary moment in which everything in intellectual life is in the process of being discussed, negotiated, and remade—and where the artist is present to watch and to participate.

This is everyone's fantasy. To be present at the moment, the gloriously and unabashedly anachronistic moment, of the making and remaking of the disciplines. To be part of what Robert Maynard Hutchins, almost fifty years ago, and describing a rather different intellectual and political project, called "The Great Conversation."[66]

"It seems to me," Dilthey reflected, interpreting his own dream, "that the time is past when there can be an independent philosophy of art, religion, law, or of the state." Dilthey's critical approach to history and to humanistic studies is vital to what we would now call "interdisciplinarity."[67]

If the humanities have a future, and I fervently believe they do, it will be a future like this one, a future that involves going back to the past, and inhabiting that predisciplinary interdisciplinary moment. Not to do away with history or historicizing or context or culture, but rather to do the opposite: to see that Freud was righter than he knew when he imagined the human mind as being like the city of Rome, layer built upon layer, each cohabiting with, not replacing, the past. Our task as scholars is to reimagine the boundaries of what we have come to believe are disciplines and to have the courage to rethink them. For as a member of any discipline comes to realize sooner or later, it's hard to know where discipline envy, like inspiration, will strike next.

3

TERMS OF ART

How widespread is infelicity?

—J. L. AUSTIN

JUXTAPOSITION and context are everything.

Readers of the *New York Times* in March 1999 had a good chance to test out the truth of this assertion as they settled in with their coffee and the morning paper. On the editorial page, in the letters column, under the banner headline "Academic Jargon Is a Cover," those interested would have found a series of letters, ranging from the dismissive to the vituperative, responding to an Arts & Ideas feature article called "Bad Writing" in the academy.[1] A professor of sociology from the University of Massachusetts at Amherst accused prominent scholars of obscurantism and self-aggrandizement. A Berkeley professor of art history retorted that critics of these academic stars should survey their own writing for "limpid sententiousness" and self-satisfied "moralisms and banalities," which were, in his view, far worse than "genuinely exploratory neologisms." "Gibberish" was a popular term among the naysayers, as was the trendiest of dismissive words, "trendy."[2]

If, however, our reader of the morning *Times*, wearying of this jousting and defensiveness, had set aside section A of the newspaper (containing "hard news" and editorials) and picked up for edification section B, "The Arts," he or she would have encountered another point of view on the question of difficulty in language. For on the first page of this section the long-time book reviewer Christopher Lehmann-Haupt was also taking note of neologisms and extreme syntactical complexity.

Lehmann-Haupt had popped a recording of a BBC radio production in the tape deck of his car and was "immediately struck by how nearly incomprehensible some of the language was." The tape was full of "confounding passages," so difficult that he could not imagine a first-time listener could ever catch the meaning. He himself had to go over and over the text, in what he characterized as "an obsessive manner," until the meanings of certain lines "revealed themselves." In search of clarification, he went questing for a written transcription, and "whenever [he] came to a difficult passage, [he] would study the notes and keep rereading it until it more or less made sense." But instead of finding this experience infuriating, he found it "gratifying," and, finally, cathartic. What was this hard text, full of "extraneous" and idiosyncratic forms? Forms that, once deciphered, led the reader to translate what he read into more straightforward terms (like "the statement simply means that love isn't real when it gets mixed up with irrelevancies")? It was Shakespeare's *King Lear.*[3]

Now, it is not my purpose to compare the philosophical writing of Judith Butler, a professor of rhetoric, or the postcolonial theory of Homi Bhabha, a professor of English, the two principal subjects of the piece on "Bad Writing," with the plays of Shakespeare. I teach all three with pleasure, and my students find reading them all, in different ways, difficult and rewarding. What I do want to emphasize, however, is that it is possible to consider a difficult text to be worth the trouble of deciphering it, and its difficulty may in fact be *part of the experience of reading*.

The topic of this chapter is that most ridiculed of all academic habits, speaking in "jargon." What is jargon, and why are they saying such terrible things about it?

They've been saying them, incidentally, for centuries: the fabled (and vilified) "jargon of the schools" has earned the public, published disrespect of such worthies as John Locke, Matthew Prior, John Pomfret, and William Cowper.[4] "Schools" in this phrase means "Schoolmen," medieval philosophers who attempted to synthesize a Christian system of logic and philosophy based on Aristotle and other ancient authors.

Hampered by bad translations of classical texts—often poor Latin rendered from questionable Arabic versions of the original Greek—and constrained as well by the necessity of pleasing the Church, the Schoolmen became proverbial, however fairly or unfairly, for quibbling and hair splitting, endlessly debating methodology and terminology. The Tudor humanist educator John Colet thought their language was barbarous and should rather be called "blotterature thenne litterature."[5] That this is a popular conception of today's scholars and university professors in the humanities will not have escaped most readers' notice, unless they live in a secluded hideaway without books, magazines, cable, or access to the Internet.

Jargon

"The perfection of style is to be clear without being mean," wrote Aristotle in his *Poetics*. To avoid "meanness," to achieve a diction that is "lofty and raised above the commonplace," writers use "unusual words," he says with approbation. "By unusual I mean strange (or rare) words, metaphorical, lengthened—anything, in short, that differs from the normal idiom." He continues:

> A diction that is made up of strange (or rare) terms is a jargon. A certain infusion . . . of these elements is necessary in style, for the strange (or rare) word, the metaphorical, the ornamental will raise it above the commonplace and mean. . . . [N]othing contributes more to produce a clearness of diction that is remote from commonness than the lengthening, contraction, and alteration of words. For by deviating in exceptional cases from the normal idiom, the language will gain distinction; while, at the same time, the partial conformity with usage will give perspicuity. The critics, therefore, are in error who censure these licenses of speech, and hold the author up to ridicule.[6]

The word "jargon" here is the choice of the translator, S. H. Butcher, in a widely used version of the text. Another respected modern translation gives the same word as "barbarism," a literal version of the Greek *barbarismos*, "foreign," which was to say, non-Greek.[7]

I will return later to this question of "foreign words" and their relation to the cry of "jargon!" For now, though, I want

simply to reemphasize the fact that Aristotle favors an author's use of a moderate proportion of "unfamiliar words" in
order to render the style "distinguished and non-prosaic,"
and that the use of "lengthened, curtailed, and altered forms
of words" is in fact *recommended* rather than discouraged or
condemned.[8] Some modicum of "jargon" (or "barbarism"),
then, can be a good thing, rescuing the style from flatness,
keeping the listener alert.

Does a jargon mean too much or too little? Does it communicate too precisely or not at all? Convey "meaning" or obfus-
cate it? Much depends upon who is doing the speaking (or
writing) and the listening (or reading).[9]

Today we have drug dealers' jargon, phone company jargon, garage jargon, theatrical jargon, collectors' jargon,
radio jargon, space jargon, political jargon, defense jargon
(a.k.a Pentagonese), nuclear jargon, Scientology jargon,
New Age jargon—you name it. And jargons are always changing. Take restaurant jargon, for example. A book on the *Jargon of Professions* observed (in 1978) that "Twenty or thirty
years ago . . . fish was upgraded to seafood."[10] These days, as
a friend pointed out to me, *seafood* sounds downmarket and
unappealing, while *fish* is the classier word, preferred by chefs
and menu writers.

Unfamiliar expressions are not always resisted; sometimes
they are a source of attraction in themselves. Sometimes, in
fact, it's the jargon itself that is the most captivating thing
about a profession or sect.[11] When I picked up a book called
Biz-Talk 1: American Business Slang and Jargon, I expected it to
be a comic send-up. Instead it was a serious usage tome, a
book of language instruction, with sections on "General Of-

fice Slang," "Computer Slang," "Meeting/Negotiation Jargon," "Business Travel Jargon," "Marketing Jargon," "Finance Slang & Jargon," and "Sports Terms Used in Business." "Jargon" in these titles had no pejorative connotation; it simply meant "essential vocabulary."

On the whole, however, popular books of jargon tend to be satirical rather than admiring. Here is the table of contents of a little volume published in 1975 called *The D.C. Dialect: How to Master the New Language of Washington in Ten Easy Lessons*:[12]

Lesson 1: Be Impersonal
Lesson 2: Be Obscure
Lesson 3: Be Pompous
Lesson 4: Be Evasive
Lesson 5: Be Repetitious
Lesson 6: Be Awkward
Lesson 7: Be Incorrect
Lesson 8: Be Faddish
Lesson 9: Be Serious
Lesson 10: Be Unintelligible

Like all such "period" documents, this one is a cultural goldmine—or minefield, depending on your point of view. The authors list a glossary of selected words and phrases in both English and "D.C. Dialect." Although they are intended to strike the reader with the ludicrousness of the coined terms, these phrases (*executive privilege* for *total immunity; independent recollection* for *memory*) now seem rather to be catalogues of normal, everyday speech. A few examples given in the book, such as *lifestyle* (instead of *life*) and *news media* (instead of *magazines*) seem particularly dated as signs of linguistic decay.

This, indeed, is one of the key things about jargon: that since language is a living thing, yesterday's jargon words may very well be today's normal or standard speech.

Neologisms, new words, are often described as jargon and therefore disparaged, especially if they play fast and loose with established parts of speech (a noun becomes a verb, a verb or an adjective turns into a noun). Jacques Derrida's portmanteau word *différance* and Homi Bhabha's revival of the little-used nineteenth-century word *hybridity* are two examples, both of which have been regularly mocked for their novelty.

But yesterday's neologisms, like yesterday's jargon, are often today's essential vocabulary. Consider a lively coinage like *virtuecrat*, first used by journalists in the early 1990s to describe, with compact irony, a public figure who makes a point of professing moral beliefs as a cultural imperative.[13] Other recent portmanteau words that may have some staying power include *micromanage* and *infomercial*, both of which characterize ways of doing business that are themselves crossover in style. (*Portmanteau* used in this sense is a Lewis Carroll term, based on the word for valise or carrying case: " 'Slithy' means 'lithe and slimy,' " Humpty Dumpty explains to Alice. "You see it's like a portmanteau—there are two meanings packed up into one word.")[14] Earlier examples of this same useful conflating tendency include *brunch*, which dates from the 1890s, and *motel*, from the 1920s. *Meritocracy, impressionism*, and *formalism* were all terms of contempt when they were first introduced. As indeed was *neologism* itself, which first ap-

peared at the very end of the eighteenth century, already
under a cloud ("Disfigured by neology, corruption, and barbarous modes of speech"), though it was later welcomed as
a nice change from "the barrenness of our Saxon" by the
English man of letters Isaac Disraeli, a descendant of Vene-
tian and Sephardic Jews. Disraeli, the father of the statesman
and novelist Benjamin Disraeli, suggested that it was the most
refined minds that produced neologisms: his exemplars were
Plato, Montaigne, and Richardson.[15]

Here are some other words that have entered the English
language as coinages or neologisms: *label*, as a verb (to affix
a name or description to); *lapse*, as a verb (to slip or fall into
error); *dialogue*, as a verb (to express in dialogue, to con-
verse—very frequently vilified, especially when associated
with pop psychology, personnel management, and "therapy-
speak"); *design*, *accused*, and *addiction*, as nouns (e.g., "the accused," the person charged with an offense); *rival*, as both
adjective and verb; *anchovy, grovel, laughable,* and *amazement.*
All these words, and at least fifteen hundred more (*traditional, excitement, protesters, circumstantial, launder, assassination,*
etc.) were introduced into written English by William Shakespeare. It's been calculated that one in twelve of Shakespeare's words were "new words"—words he introduced, invented, popularized, or radically altered.[16] Could we imagine
doing without them?

Before we condemn jargon, we should take a longer view
(what linguists would call, in their jargon, a "diachronic"
view) across history, to see how frequently one generation's
jargon becomes another's ordinary usage.

We might take as our first example the very word in question here: jargon. A "jargon" was once a cipher or secret
code, used, for example, by spies, mystics, great personages
(the king, queen, and "great men of the realm"), and—in
one cited instance—a deaf child, who communicated by
means of "a sort of Jargon in which she could hold conversation." It was, in short, insider language, a language designed,
or functioning, to keep outsiders out. This is still one meaning of the term. In the early twentieth century, the word *jargon* in German was sometimes used to mean "Yiddish." Thus
Franz Kafka writes in his diary that he has delivered "a little
introductory lecture on Yiddish [*einen kleinen Einleitungsvortrag über Jargon*]," and refers to the Yiddish theater, in a letter
to his fiancée, as "das Jargontheater."[17]

"Jargon" once meant the inarticulate chattering of birds.
Chaucer and Gower use it in this way, and modern literature
has revived this sense of twittering utterance. In birds it is
usually a pleasant trait, not only melodious but also social:
Coleridge's Ancient Mariner enthused about the way "little
birds" seemed to fill the sea and air "with their sweet jargoning!" and the "jargon" and "jargoning" of canaries, snowbirds, and indeed singing insects like cicadas is often described as delightful or sweet.[18]

But what is soothing and sociable in birds (or cicadas) may
be irritating in persons. The "jargon of the schools" is often
described by its critics as "noisy" and "sounding." When unintelligibility crosses the line from the charming to the opaque,
nonsensical, "barbarous," or "meaningless," tempers get
short. So *jargon* from the time of Chaucer has also meant
"unintelligible or meaningless talk or writing; nonsense, gib-

berish" (here *The Oxford English Dictionary*, in a burst of editorial commentary, adds "often a term of contempt for something the speaker does not understand").[19] Thus alchemy, religion, theology, and tax laws are all dismissed, by various seventeenth-, eighteenth-, and nineteenth-century detractors, as "mere Jargon and Imposture" or "mere jargon and insignificant non-sence." In fact *mere* is probably still the most common intensifier for *jargon*—a sign of deprecation and dismissal.

And indeed, the matter of "contempt" moves from the status of a parenthetical aside to full frontal visibility with the definition that most closely fits our modern understanding of what "jargon" is and who dislikes it.

> *jargon*, sb. 6. Applied contemptuously to any mode of speech abounding in unfamiliar terms, or peculiar to a particular set of persons, as the language of scholars or philosophers, the terminology of a science or art, or the cant of a class, sect, trade, or profession.

So jargon words in this sense are professional words: terms of art.

And to resist jargon is to protest against professionalism, professionalization, professions—and, not incidentally, professors.

Terms of Art

The phrase *term of art* is by now so relatively quaint in our society that it has become—there is no other word for it—a term of art. That is to say, a technical term, a word or phrase "peculiar to, or having a peculiar use in, a particular art or pursuit."

Even in earlier years, terms of art were regarded with suspicion. For every fairly neutral reference (an 1807 book entitled *Explanation of the Terms of Art in Anatomy,* a mention of "The Termes and Words of Art" by the jurist Edward Coke), there is another that breathes a grumpy sense of coinage, neologism, duplicity, and pretense. "A few thumping blustering terms of art," Sir Walter Scott thumps and blusters (in *The Antiquary*). In 1701 Jonathan Swift satirized new words that end, fashionably, in *–ize.* We may well say that nothing changes.[20]

Terms of art, then, are not only artisanal but artful, crafty—and, more often than not, ostentatious and false. Even in the *real* olden days, that is, in the time of Chaucer, such "termes" were associated with the arts of astrology, alchemy, and law.[21] Recall that astrology and alchemy were popular and respected "scientific" professions as late as the midseventeenth century, when a formal Society of Astrology was founded with a membership of about forty, predating by a decade the founding of the Royal Society. And each art had its set of terms.

We can see hints of the intoxication with magical, abstruse terminology—terms of art—in today's televised medical dramas, when the cries of "Pulse-ox!" "Tube 'im!" and "Stat!" give an aura of entirely spurious authenticity, while TV doctors offering highly technical explanations are brusquely interrupted, in midphrase, by patients or family members demanding that they speak plain English. For the audience, though—and also for the patients—it's partly the medical mumbo-jumbo that creates the respect. The same goes for legal dramas and even police stories. Jargon has its pleasures.

Nor has the phrase *term of art* disappeared today. It's still regularly used by lawyers and other professionals. In the early days of the House Judiciary Committee's discussion of impeachment proceedings against President Clinton, the chief investigative counsel for the Republicans disputed the importance of Monica Lewinsky's assertion that no one had asked her to lie in her affidavit in the Paula Jones case. "No one asked her to tell the truth, either," he said. "Based on my reading of the record, 'no one asked me to lie' is a term of art."[22]

But the best discussion of this curious phrase may be found in David Mamet's play *Oleanna*, which begins with a wonderful send-up of the term *term of art*. At the beginning of the play, John, a young and rather pompous sociology professor, is on the telephone with his wife, discussing the house they hope to buy. But a problem has arisen with an "easement" across the land, and John demands to know whether *easement* is a term of art: are they bound by it? Sitting in his office and overhearing his conversation is Carol, the student who, though she seems docile to a fault, will come to be his nemesis. When he hangs up, she asks him, "What is a 'term of art'"? He is taken aback and, like many another professor caught out in this situation, he stalls.

> JOHN: What is a "term of art"? It seems to mean a *term*, which has come, through its use, to mean something *more specific* than the words would, to someone *not acquainted* with them . . . indicate. That, I believe, is what a "term of art" would mean. (*Pause*)

CAROL: You don't know what it means . . . ?

JOHN: I'm not sure that I know what it means. It's one of those things, perhaps you've had them, that you look them up, or have someone explain them to you, and you say "aha," and you immediately *forget* what . . .[23]

Since *easement*, in real estate law, means "the right or privilege of using something not one's own," which is what John will ultimately, in a way, be accused of doing in this play about language and a claim of sexual harassment, Mamet is having his little joke with us. An earlier meaning of *easement*, "to give or get relief from pain or discomfort," is the reason Carol seems to have come to her professor's office, but by the end of the play each of them will wind up attacking the other, with catastrophic results for the smug and clueless John. In effect, Mamet takes the term *term of art* and returns it from real estate to writing, from law to literature. To what we would call "art."

The word *jargon*, when used to describe and dismiss the language of critical theory in the humanities, is in fact describing what for practitioners of those disciplines are terms of art. The quarrel is often picked over vocabulary and syntax, but what is at issue, very often, is not language usage but the legitimacy of critical theory as a discipline.

Academic Jargon

Which kinds of linguistic formations are identified and condemned today as "academic jargon"? In scholarly writing, the chief culprits seem to be what might be called "transformers":

nouns that are turned into verbs, sometimes but not always via the much despised *ize* suffix (e.g., *problematize*, but also *reference*) and adjectives that become nouns (*the ethical, the other, the abject; the Imaginary, the Symbolic, and the Real*). Also on the hit list: proper names that become adjectives (*Adornian, Althusserian, Foucauldian, Barthesian, post-Fordist*), as if they referred to adherents of a sect. *Freudian* and *Marxist* have long been hurled about as labels, with greater or lesser accuracy. But do we object to *Jeffersonian?* or *Lincolnesque?* Jargon, as always, is in the ear of the listener.

It's not only scholars, of course, who play with parts of speech in this way. A *New York Times* article on changes wrought by Web culture remarked that *creative* is now a noun, replacing *writer* ("she's the creative on this project"), and *workshop* is now a verb, replacing *writing* ("I'm workshopping my novel"). When a Web author, asked for a term to replace *episodes* in a forthcoming dramatic series, suggested the word *chapters*, she was rebuked for being "so print" and "very old media."[24] In the "new media," as we might call them, such coinages are part of the business.

But when scholars and critics invent vocabulary, they are often severely judged. Thus we hear of "The pseudo-metaphysical jargon that gets by as art criticism."[25] Or, in a particularly felicitous phrase about supposed infelicity, "The refingered worry-beads of lit-crit jargon."[26] These, incidentally, are quotations from the late sixties and early seventies, not from yesterday or the day before.

Architectural criticism has been one recent site of complaint, with accusations of "designer babble" being leveled by such luminaries as the former editor of *Architectural Record*,

Steven A. Kliment. "It's enough to make you fear for the future of the profession," declared a *New York Times* reporter, who dutifully reprinted offending passages Kliment had singled out from architectural journals. "When you start talking about decontextualizing your intrinsic modularity," the reporter declared, "you know your profession's in trouble linguistically."

But what profession did he mean? The writers "decontextualized" for this "shame on you" piece were architectural historians and critics, not architects presenting designs to their clients.[27] They were writing for each other, in terms borrowed and expanded from other art, literature, and philosophy criticism of our time. Like all such "aren't they silly?" articles—the journalistic equivalent of TV "blooper shows," quick to assemble and often wickedly amusing—this one revealed as much about the profession of journalism as about the profession of architectural history.

As we've already noted, *academic* is one of the harshest things you can say about books written for popular and mainstream audiences, while *journalistic* is the kiss of death for scholarly writing. Both epithets misunderstand and underestimate the pleasures of precise and colorful style, as well as the intimate relation between the terms through which one thinks and the very possibility of thought.

Of course, academics have been under attack and under surveillance for their bad language for a long time now. *Academic*, as a noun denoting a college or university professor, is itself a jargon term used only by "nonacademics." Professors tend to call themselves professors, or teachers, or scholars. But *academic*, as an epithet, seems to combine implications of (undeserved) privilege with implications of (fully deserved) irrelevance. This last is yet another two-edged sword, since the only thing worse than an irrelevant academic is a "relevant" one, one who panders, or so it is claimed, to popular ideas and current political concerns.

In fact, *academic* is a word that is split from the beginning into associations of honor and blame. It often goes along with social awkwardness on the one hand (Dr. Johnson referred to his "academick rudeness") and intellectual skepticism on the other (David Hume remarked that: "The wise lend a very academic faith to every report which favours the passion of the reporter").[28] Thus the word *academic* in modern parlance has come to mean artificial or impractical, merely theoretical (as in "only of academic interest") or excessively formal (as in "academic painting"). *An* "academic" could be an ancient philosopher of the school of Plato or a senior member of a university or a member of a society for promoting art or science, like the Royal Academy or the American Academy of Arts and Letters. But *academic* as both a noun and an adjective is not really a term of high repute in today's world. In fact the use of *academic* to describe a scholar, like the use of *deconstructionist* to describe a literary critic, might be regarded as a failure of the "Shibboleth" test.

Shibboleth, you will recall, was a word used by Jephthah in the Book of Judges to distinguish the fleeing Ephraimites (who pronounced *sh* the same as *s*), from his own men the Gileadites (Judges 12:4–6). If a man denied that he was an Ephraimite, he was told to pronounce the word, and if he said "Sibboleth," they took him and slew him. *Shibboleth* thus came to mean a word used as a test for detecting foreigners and also, by extension, a catchword used by a party or sect to identify members and exclude outsiders.[29] In this sense academic jargon itself functions as a kind of shibboleth. While those who can't pronounce or use it are not slain, it is sometimes contended that they are not read or promoted either. In a "publish or perish" profession, one can perish by the word rather than by the sword.

A Report from the Trenches

Popular linguist Mario Pei once asked a group of graduate students in English at Seton Hall University to give him, "individually and without collusion," their personal lists of five beautiful and five ugly words, along with five coinages of words they would like to see and five words they thought should be dropped from the language. The results were instructive. "Ugly words," Pei reported, tended to be "monosyllabic and of native origin" (*loot, snooze, retch, jazz, gut, brat, wrench*). "Beautiful" words included a number of foreign forms (*Zeitgeist, Weltanschauung, anthropos, Lorelei*), and many he characterized as "polysyllabic forms of obviously foreign and learned origin" (including *sonorous, epidermal, lugubrious, superfluous, opalescent, scintillating, caricature, aphorism, platitude, evanescence, nefarious, tantalize*).

Words suggested for the discard pile, he noted, may have been colored by their meanings; among those cited were *Lesbian, lukewarm, momism, humanoid, niggardly, poetess, authoress, fantastic, colossal,* and *mastermind.* Coinages, predictably, were the most inventive: *boron,* for a boring person; *mutatophobia,* for fear of change; and one of my own favorites, *antiquidate.*

What was most interesting in this set of responses was the lack of fear of foreign words and words with Latinate or other complex formations.

But Pei's survey, I thought, might be a little out of date, since it was undertaken almost thirty years ago.

I decided, therefore, to repeat the experiment.

My own "focus group" was also made up of graduate students in English, and the first thing I can say is that it's obviously impossible to generalize from this small and unscientific sample. Some respondents showed clear aural preferences (one respondent's "beautiful" words all had soft *e* sounds—*caramel, dwell, wend, trellis;* another's, soft *i*'s—*lilt, iridescent, mellifluous*). Many expressed uncertainty as to whether the "beauty" ought to inhere in the sound or the meaning, though among the words deemed especially attractive were some rather unbeautiful concepts, like *Ebola, diarrhea,* and *syphilis.* Most surprising to me among the "beauties" was *analog.* The ugly words included, predictably, some racial epithets and some diseases, but also several journalistic abbreviations (*burb* for *suburb, temp* for *temporary employee, HMO*). Two different students objected to *pulchritudinous,* and one of these had chosen as "beautiful" a couple of words with very similar sounds: *lugubrious* and *lucubration.*

But it was with the coinages and the expungeables that we hit pay dirt. Among the gems in the former category: *glambiguous* (meaning "glamorously ambiguous"), *frusturpation* defined by its originator as "anger and discomfort caused by writer's block"—these were, after all, graduate students), *tech-nophallus* (presumably a term of empowerment for computer jocks), *evailable* (reachable by e-mail), *binge-reading*. Most of the coinages, as these will suggest, were picturesque, imaginative, metaphorical. But a few were additions to the literary or cultural critic's toolbox: my favorite of these was the eloquently compact *trans-rational*.

What words did these contemporary graduate students in English want to banish from the language? Mostly terms from tabloid journalism, computer-speak, middle management, the so-called "helping professions," and advertising. They wanted to put closure to *closure*, to slam the gate on all words ending in *-gate* (*travelgate, Monica-gate*), to get rid of *impact* as a verb, *disconnect* as a noun, *proactive, mission statement, incentivize, utilize, codependent, enabler, SUV, significant other, legalese, computerese, hypertext, workfare, contingency, telecommute,* and *networking*. Two wanted to banish *deplane*. The only terms from literary and cultural analysis that were considered prime candidates for disposal were *subaltern, left-wing, right-wing,* and *race*. (Though one medievalist protested against the use of *medieval* to mean "primitive" or "barbaric.")

It would be foolhardy to draw "scientific" (or even "social-scientific") conclusions from these responses. But in the most general way they do tell us something about jargon. For what seemed to be desired were words that were precise, on the one hand, and striking—even witty—on the other. What was *not* desired were words that seemed to be euphemisms, sound bites, or facile usages spawned by cyber culture.

Incidentally, I deliberately omitted from my set of questions the word *jargon*, which I thought would produce some knee-jerk responses. After the survey I wrote back to my respondents and asked them to send me some words they considered jargon. Among the replies: *negotiate, boundaries, liminal, theory, downsize, escrow, Fannie Mae, URL, historicist,* and a range of typographical practices, from subtitles given after a colon to parentheses and virgules ("slash marks"). From which we deduce that some of my students are looking for mortgages, others are grappling with the Internet, and more than a few are tired of terms they encounter so often in literary-critical writing that they have lost their freshness, and therefore some of their meaning.

And this brings us to something we might call "the jargon effect."

The Jargon Effect

The jargon effect is a sign that something intrinsic to the discipline is happening at two different points along the critical continuum. First, among theorists and scholars who coin new terms or formulations so as to make headway on difficult problems within the discipline. And second, among apprentices to the discipline (graduate students, medical students, law students, and law review editors who use these new terms as their point of entry into disciplinary thinking).

Michel Foucault called those nineteenth-century authors who became particularly influential in twentieth-century theory "initiators of discursive practices." He acknowledged his own jargon by putting that phrase in quotation marks: "somewhat arbitrarily, we might call them 'initiators of discursive practices.'" Foucault asserted that Marx and Freud made possible "not only a certain number of analogies that could be adopted by future texts" but also "a certain number of differences." They were not simply authors of specific books and essays; "they both established the endless possibility of discourse." Words like *unconscious* and *ideology* took on new life after they used them. These "initiators," like the "genius" described by Kant, set things in motion: "they produced not only their own work but the possibility and the rules of formation of other texts."[30]

What has happened in literary critical language, I think, is that the "de-familiarized" has become overly familiar, has sometimes become, as we like to say, a trope or gesture. Such stylistic innovations have become clichés, dead metaphors. The first time I saw the word *(en)gendering*, or indeed the word *(re)membering*, the curious typography probably made me think twice about how gender, or memory, come into being. That gender is a process, not just a "fact of life." Or that memories are, by their very nature, developed backward from "now" to "then," and may bear a trace of fantasy, idealization, projection, or some other mental editing technique of which I am not fully conscious. All of this I might have derived from the orthographic trick of separating these familiar words into prefix and root by the use of parentheses. But the third time or the thirtieth time I saw these words written in this form, the device had become stale: it no longer made me stop and think.

Resentment of jargon comes from several sources, as we have already seen: resistance to being left out of an in-group conversation; fear (often transmuted, as a defense mechanism, into dislike or even hatred) of what is not understood or recognized; suspicion that something subversive may be going on, enabled by a code or cipher; and, on the other hand—if it is indeed another hand—aesthetic recoil at language that is perceived as ugly, pretentious, or anomalous.

Nonetheless, I want to insist here that jargon is language in action, or rather, that jargon is a sign that something is happening in language.

We might note that when poets engage in such coinages and rearrangements of syntax, what they are said to produce is not "jargon" but "difficulty," something often valued rather than disparaged.[31] It is an old argument to say that the critic and the scholar should aim at the same precision of language as the poet. But it is a good argument still. We need to distinguish, on the one hand, between the creative use of language and the parroting of terms; but also, on the other, between the arbitrary dismissal of new language forms in one genre and the celebration of those new forms in another.

Theodor Adorno addressed this question with characteristic verve in *Minima Moralia,* under the rubric of "Morality and Style": "Vague expression permits the hearer to imagine whatever suits him and what he already thinks in any case. Rigorous formulation demands unequivocal comprehension, conceptual effort, to which people are deliberately disencouraged. . . . Only what they do not need first to understand, they consider understandable; only the word coined by commerce, and really alienated, touches them as familiar." For Adorno, this unhappy state of affairs contributed in a major way to "the demoralization of intellectuals." His response was to throw down a gauntlet, insisting that "Those who would escape it must recognize the advocates of communicability as traitors to what they communicate."[32]

This seems to me an unnecessarily dire view. Rigorous formulation need not preclude clarity; difficulty and obscurity are not by definition the same. The difficulty of expressing complex ideas in accessible language might itself be an appealing challenge to intellectuals who want to resist demoralization. Indeed, this was also Adorno's opinion: "the thicket is no sacred grove. There is a duty to clarify all difficulties that result merely from esoteric complacency." It is precisely a sense of the complacency of insider terms that often riles noninitiates reading academic prose, together with an intuition that such terms, too, can be "words coined by commerce," the passwords to the portals of professional advancement. Yet it is a salient fact that academic departments of "communications" are often located in schools of journalism and/or schools of information management, not in liberal arts or humanities programs. "Rhetoric" departments may be principally concerned either with philosophy and critical theory or, far more commonly, with composition and public speaking. When communication and rhetoric are themselves professionally defined as modes of mass culture, the issue of what is or is not jargon shifts: the question then becomes not how to avoid "jargon," but how to keep language at once precise and rich. The term *creative writing* has become a virtual synonym for fiction, drama, and poetry, when it might well stand as a model for all discursive language, especially that produced by scholars whose medium is ideas.

In Fashion

Fad, fashionable, and *trendy* are about the most damning epithets that can be hurled at ideas these days. Each connotes
breeziness, unseriousness, evanescence. *Fashionable* is usually
intended as an insult, and manages to connote at once the
status of slavish follower (cf. "fashion victim," or "slave to fashion") and an upper-class, or wanna-be upper-class, snooti-
ness: fashionable novels, fashionable gossip, fashionable
clothing and pastimes. When *fashionable* is connected to ideas
or to words, it is therefore often dismissive, as in the following
examples cited by the *Oxford English Dictionary*:

- From the eighteenth-century author Lord Chesterfield:
  "Taste is now the fashionable Word of the fashionable
  World."
- From the *Listener* in 1962: "The phrase 'built-in obsoles-
  cence' . . . was very fashionable, especially among cynics,
  about ten years ago."
- From the *Times* of London in 1982: "'Ageism' is a new word
  in the lexicon of fashionable evils."

There is also, of course, the title of Sokal and Bricmont's
book, *Fashionable Nonsense: Postmodern Intellectuals' Abuse of
Science* (originally published in French as *Impostures intel-
lectuelles*), in which the first four words are all, in effect, terms
of abuse.

Fashionable words decried for their fashionableness often,
incidentally, meet the usual fate of useful new terms and a
generation later are absorbed into the language as if they

had always been there. It is rather charming to find that the word *autograph* was regarded in 1808 as a piece of "modern fashionable literary nomenclature." And the same is true for ideas. Pragmatism, described in 1906 as "the most recent and (philosophically speaking) fashionable 'ism' that the new century has produced" is no longer new (though it's again newly "fashionable"). The complaint aired in the *Times Literary Supplement* of 1958 against "Fashionable art critics' jargon which attributes organic qualities to Mr. [Henry] Moore's bronzes or Mr. Frank Lloyd Wright's pillars of Pyrex glass" describes a kind of criticism that could be read today as tolerably old-fashioned.[33]

Another quality of *fashionable* is that it is always, it seems, hurled from the right toward the (supposed) left: thus one might have read, in 1968, of "the demolition of fashionable McLuhanite myths about television" and in 1974 that "It's fashionable nowadays to 'knock' England for its shortcomings." Arthur Koestler claimed that "The most fashionable poet among the snobs and parlor-Communists of the period was Bertolt Brecht." No less a word pundit than George Orwell was expressing utmost when he wrote, in 1945, about a recent "counter-attack against the rather shallow Leftism which was fashionable in the previous decade."[34] Though it would be hypothetically conceivable to speak of the "rather shallow Rightism" of the decade previous to the present one, it's unlikely that such a political position would be characterized as "fashionable," though it certainly was.

Fad, a term that became popular late in the nineteenth century, is often taken to denote a craze or hobby: the mambo, the twist, the zoot suit, colored cigarettes, hula hoops, streak-

ing and panty raids (all examples given in the *OED*). So fad
too is dismissive: kid stuff. When C. S. Lewis wrote that one
should "Beware of . . . 'neo-scholasticism' as a fad," he clearly
did not intend a compliment. But as the *Nation* noted in 1910,
"The fad of today is the orthodoxy of tomorrow."[35]

As for *trend* and *trendy*, also often used dismissively, they
derive, ironically enough, from the social science practice of
"trend analysis." Yet the culprits accused of "trendiness" are
more often than not humanists. A trend in economics, psychology, or statistics can be taken seriously: it is measurable
and mappable. But rendered into an adjective or applied to
ideas or to culture, "trend" becomes whim—or worse, cynical
opportunism ("trendy clergy trying to introduce so-called up-
to-date forms of worship"). This double standard, that up-to-
date-ness is often good in scientists, bad in humanists, un-
derpins the negative uses of all three of these terms. Though
there are exceptions to this disciplinary divide, as in this un-
kind cut from the *Lancet*: "Pathobiology (a trendy name for
general pathology) seems to be a fashionable subject in the
United States."[36]

How long does a "trend" (or "fad," or "fashion") have to
be in place for it to transcend its suspect status? Could we
talk of the "trend" toward monotheism over the past several
thousand years? Or the "trend" among the middle and
upper-middle classes toward raising one's children at home,
rather than farming them out to wet-nurses or local poor
families or sending them off to boarding school at an early
age? For that matter, are we prepared to discuss jargon terms
like *born-again* and *personal savior* as "fashionable" signs of a
"trendy" upsurge in evangelical Christianity? These phrases

are certainly jargon by almost any definition, since they are insider terms that telescope a series of complex ideas into a concise expression. But though there may indeed be a trend toward publicly avowed Christian faith, it is unlikely to be called "trendy," since that would imply impermanence and lack of respect.

Consider also the peculiar fate of *political correctness*, a jargon term if there ever was one. Used with heavy self-irony by the left in the 1970s as a kind of amused reality check on its own excesses, and often abbreviated by its initials as a sign of this affectionate self-estrangement (as in, "Oh, don't be so P.C.!"), the term was picked up by the right, denuded of any soupçon of irony, and used as a club to beat those very persons who had coined it to begin with.[37] Whose jargon is "political correctness," the left's or the right's? Bear in mind that *left* and *right* are themselves jargon or cultural shorthand, derived from seating positions within the French Assembly— a long-dead metaphor with lots of life in it. *P.C.* is an object lesson here. There's a danger in any clever coinage, one with which journalists have again been sometimes unwittingly complicit, since the double back-flip that makes some critical terms useful in literary theory has to be flattened out for public consumption. The most misused word, by far, is *deconstruct*, used all the time as a verb to mean "destroy" or "pull down" or "take to pieces," a misunderstanding that pairs it, all too neatly, with the frequent charge of *nihilism* (another misunderstood term). As we've seen, to *deconstruct* in literary or philosophical analysis is to analyze, not to destroy.[38] But *deconstruct*, though it is properly defined as "a method of analyzing texts" in modern reference books, is very often used incorrectly, as in this heartfelt denunciation of modern life by a letter writer to the *Arizona Republic:* "our media culture, which snickers at hard work, ridicules character and devalues human life as it deconstructs societal norms."[39] The implication here is not that the media are *exploring* societal norms, but rather that they are *undermining* or *destroying* them. And this sense of the word has become so widespread that, as with political correctness, it's pointless to try to correct it. That, paradoxically, is one way language grows.

There may be another small irony in the fact that "media culture," not "academia," is blamed for this breakdown of values. The mainstreaming of academic words is not something scholars themselves could ever achieve. The fact is that *political correctness* and *deconstruction* are nice juicy terms, ripe for reuse and abuse. On the "any publicity is good publicity" principle, literary scholars should perhaps welcome these appropriations, or at any rate accept them. A coiner of critical terms can no more control the meanings and inflections those terms acquire elsewhere than the author of a poem can control the reader's interpretations.

Foreign Words

Not too long ago, the very mark of learnedness and cosmopolitan sophistication in academic lecturing was to ornament one's talk with snatches of quotation in many languages. Needless to say, the languages were European, and the quotations went untranslated. Understanding them—and knowing

their sources—was part of the test, the password or open sesame, of cultivated intellectual society.

This was in part, no doubt, a residual inheritance of a political necessity, for some of the most eloquent speakers in academic circles had been born and educated in Europe and had moved to the United States or to England in flight from Nazi (or Stalinist) persecution. But whatever its genesis, the practice of "language dropping" (on the model of "name dropping") hit a peak at midcentury and was to a certain extent an artifact of modernism. But today some of the animus against "academic jargon," as we've seen, comes from the "foreignness" of its words, terms, and syntactical formations—and especially its borrowings from French and German.

In fact, one of the ancillary but important factors in the tendency to deplore "theory talk" in the humanities results from translation—or perhaps I should say "under-translation." Words like *discourse, subject, interpellation,* and *hegemony,* for example, are key elements in the works of influential European thinkers like Michel Foucault and Louis Althusser. I'm informed by a friend in film studies that a popular acronym in that field is SLAB: Saussure (semiotics), Lacan (psychoanalysis), Althusser (Marxism), and Barthes (textual theory), the critics who dominated the analysis of cinema in the 1970s and 1980s. That terms from these critics are "translated" into English words that closely resemble the French (and Latin) "originals" has irked many people, who ask why literary critics can't write in "plain English."

Leaving aside for a moment the reverse trend—the importation into European languages of words that are English or American, like *le shampooing* (shampoo; i.e., the noun—the stuff you put on your hair) or *le footing* (jogging; *faire un petit footing* is to go for a little jog), a development which doesn't irritate Americans but sticks in the craw of the French Academy—let's concentrate for a moment on what might be gained by preserving these terms in their rather estranging "foreign" form. And the answer here is just that: *estrangement.*

This is a problem that was well noted by Adorno forty years ago.

> Attempts at formulation that swim against the stream of the usual linguistic splashing in order to capture the intended matter precisely, and that take pains to fit complex conceptual relationships into the framework of syntax, arouse rage because they require effort. The person who is naïve about language will ascribe the strangeness of such writing to foreign words, which he holds responsible for everything he doesn't understand even when he is quite familiar with the words. Ultimately, what is going on is largely a defense against ideas, which are imputed to the words: the blame is misdirected.[40]

Even more pointedly in another context, he observed: "German words of foreign derivation are the Jews of language."[41] We might recall Kafka's use of "jargon" as the word for "Yiddish." Although foreign words are not necessarily jargon words, they are often treated with the same suspicion.

Yet "foreign words" also have a great appeal, at least to some speakers and writers. How does Adorno explain this? Quite simply, they are erotic. "Since language is erotically charged in its words, at least for the kind of person who is capable of expression, love drives us to foreign words. In reality, it is that love that sets off the indignation over their use . . . what lures us is a kind of exogamy of language . . . foreign words made us blush, like saying the name of a secret love."[42] The contemporary substitute for foreignness in a world more vividly global may be that other erotic exotic we have had frequent opportunity to observe, the allure of scientific vocabulary.[43]

So what can foreign words do? Foreign words, Adorno suggests, "teach us that language can no longer cure us of specialization by imitating nature; it can only do so by assuming the burden of specialization."[44] And such words can "shock with their obstinacy." "Shock," he thought in 1959, "may now be the only way to reach human beings through language."

As an expatriate who worked in Hollywood and then returned to postwar Germany, Adorno was especially concerned with the nature of the German language, where, he thought, foreign words stuck out, "unassimilated," in contrast to French, where Gallic and Romance elements combined early, and English, where "the Saxon elements represent the archaic or concrete aspect and the Latin represent the civilizatory or modern aspect."

But the native English or French speaker may have a different view. In fact, the competing claims of the French and English languages have dominated the long history of culture war and sibling rivalry between these periodically incestuous nations and produced considerable angst about what I have called the jargon effect. For complaints about "foreign words" and their deleterious effect on language and national character are not a new story.

Here is an account of linguistic changes in the medieval period. At first, writes a chronicler of the Norman Conquest,

> few French words crept into English, and for most of those which did we can see a distinct reason. But, as the fusion of

races went on, as French became, not so much a foreign tongue as a fashionable tongue, the infusion of French words into English went on much faster. The love of hard words, of words which are thought to sound learned or elegant, that is, for the most part, words which are not thoroughly understood, is, I conceive, not peculiar to any one age. What it leads to in our own day we see in that foul jargon against whose inroads lovers of their native tongue have to strive. But it was busily at work in the thirteenth and fourteenth centuries.[45]

This is an English writer, voicing suspicion of the "fashionable" French in the late 1800s. (We might note again how often that word *fashionable* is used both dismissively and in connection with the influence of French culture.) Although linguistic fashions from Italy, Spain, and the Netherlands all influenced the English court and English society from the time of Elizabeth onward, introducing many neologisms that are now part of the language, for three centuries after the Norman Conquest many English writers wrote in French. In a way then, French, the near other, *had* to be viewed as a "foul jargon" in order for English to be English.

But the French, for their part, were no slackers when it came to guarding the native tongue from foreign assaults. The French Academy, founded in 1635 by Cardinal Richelieu, continues today to mount a vigorous defense against the incursion of Americanisms, gender inclusiveness, and (*quelle horreur!*) other evidences of "political correctness," the one piece of American jargon fully embraced by European language conservatives.

In England foreignness was thought to weaken a manly language. "Our own tongue should be written *clean* and *pure, unmixt* and *unmangled*," wrote Sir John Cheke to the Elizabethan translator Sir Thomas Hoby.[46] "Plain speaking" was the English way—or at least *an* English way. "I speak to thee plain soldier," says one Shakespearean figure, and another laments

> Because I cannot flatter and look fair,
> Smile in men's faces, smooth, deceive, and cog,
> Duck with French nods and apish courtesy,
> I must be held a rancorous enemy.
> Cannot a plain man live and think no harm?

The first speaker is King Henry V, formerly the artful Prince Hal, only now (artfully) turning himself into a plain, blunt Englishman to woo the French princess: "plainness," an English trait, is for him just another disguise. The second speaker, of course, is Richard III.

Various attempts have been made over the years to guard or preserve English as the French Academy does French. The Society for Pure English, a membership-only group of librarians, philologists, and literary scholars founded by poet laureate Robert Bridges, published, in the first half of this century, a series of tracts on metaphor, the split infinitive, hyphens, Oxford English, American English, "Needed Words," Notes on Relative Clauses, and Spelling Reform, among other lively topics. A very different initiative, the Plain English Campaign begun in Britain in 1979, has given us such modern classics as *Utter Drivel! A Decade of Jargon and Gobbledygook*, aiming "to encourage government departments, councils and companies to use clear language in the forms, leaflets and agreements that they ask the citizen to deal with."[47]

"In plain English" is itself a code phrase for avoiding euphemism or fancy language. Thus we find phrases like "a pelisse, which in plain English is a long cloak" and "less efficacious, that is, in plain English ineffectual," both of which body forth a good deal of what we would today call "attitude" together with their cultural translations.[48] The second of these examples sounds quite modern, but in fact it dates from the seventeenth century.

Plain English was thus tacitly or explicitly contrasted with fancy or fussy or erotically suggestive French. Curiously, but by a kind of logical extension, in the nineteenth and twentieth centuries *French*, came to mean "bad language," especially in the phrase "pardon my French!" "Damn fool," says a character in Mary McCarthy's *A Charmed Life.* "Pardon my French." A Danziger editorial cartoon imagined the response of the "Susan Faludi Fan Club" at the local VFW Hall, as a cluster of veterans collaborated on a letter to the feminist author: "Babe, you are right! We have been stiffed good! (Excuse our French.)" Among the other words "excused" in passages of twentieth-century writing with the phrase "pardon my French" (according to the *OED*) are *bloody*, *arse*, and *buggered*—none of them, needless to say, French. Each, in fact, could be called something very like "plain English."[49]

But this is to look at "plain speaking" from a particularly Anglocentric point of view. The French also have their ver-

Down at the VFW the Susan Faludi Fan Club Holds a Meeting

sion of plain speech: the famous *clarté française*, or "French clarity." "Some forms of language are forbidden to the critic as being '*jargon*,'" writes Roland Barthes in a brilliant account of the situation. "Only one form of language is allowed: '*clarity*.'"[50]

'French clarity' . . . is a jargon just like any other. It is a particular kind of language, written by a defined group of writers, critics and chroniclers; essentially it is a pastiche not even of our classical authors but only of the classicism of our writers. This backward-looking jargon is in no way shaped by precise requirements of reasoning or an ascetic absence of images, as can be the formal language of logic (it is only here that one would have the right to talk of 'clarity'), but by a community of stereotypes, . . . and of course by a refusal of certain words, rejected with horror or irony as intruders from foreign worlds, hence suspect. We have here a conservative decision to change nothing in the way that different kinds of vocabulary are marked off and shared out: it is as though language were a kind of gold rush, in which each discipline (a concept which in fact derived from the way universities organize their work) is conceded a small language territory, a sort of terminological miner's claim whose confines one cannot leave (philosophy, for example, is allowed its own jargon). The territory conceded to criticism is, however, bizarre; it is particular, since foreign words cannot be introduced into it (as if criticism had extremely small conceptual needs), yet it is nevertheless promoted to the dignity of a universal language. This universality, which is nothing but *current usage*, is faked; made up from an enormous quantity of tics and refusals, it is nothing more than yet another particular language: it is universality appropriated by the class of property owners.[51]

For Barthes, the vaunted "French clarity" was "a language whose origin is political. It was born at a time when the upper classes hoped—in accordance with a well-known ideological practice—to convert the particularity of their writing into a universal idiom, persuading people that the 'logic' of French was an absolute logic."[52] In this case, then, it was the claim of being "universal" that was political. Not, as in our current intellectual climate, the other way around.

And this brings us to a remarkable paradox that lies at the heart of the question of "jargon."

The Paradox of Jargon

In his *Essay Concerning Human Understanding* (1690), John
Locke found offense equally in the mealy-mouthed iteration
of platitudes and the pretentious coinage of new terms. Ad-
dressing "the Abuse of Words," he took to task both those
who "by an unpardonable negligence . . . familiarly use words
which the propriety of language *has* affixed to very important
ideas, without any distinct meaning at all," and those who
adopted "an *affected obscurity*," by either using old words in
new and unusual ways or introducing new and ambiguous
terms, often without defining them and in contexts that
made their meaning unclear.

Interestingly, it was to the first of these kinds of word abuse
that he applied the term *jargon*: "*Wisdom, glory, grace,* &c., are
words frequent enough in every man's mouth; but if a great
many of those who use them should be asked what they mean
by them, they would be at a stand, and not know what to
answer. . . . This insignificancy in their words, when they
come to reason either their tenets or interest, manifestly fills
their discourse with abundance of empty unintelligible noise
and jargon, especially in moral matters."[53] These moral rant-
ers are arguably more like today's virtuecrats, filling the air-
waves and news journals with calls for "character" and "values," than like the academics regularly lambasted in the
press. Although he objected just as strongly to the preten-
tiousness of the learned doctors, the word *jargon* for Locke
meant not "hard words" but empty platitudes.

The title of Theodor Adorno's book *The Jargon of Authenticity* has itself entered "the jargon" as a cant phrase. What does it mean? The book was Adorno's critique of the ideology of German existentialism, an ideology that, he believed, offered mystification in place of analysis. Writing after World War II (his book was first published in German in 1964), Adorno argued that contemporary German existentialists, writers like Martin Buber, Karl Jaspers, and Martin Heidegger, had in effect turned their philosophical terms into a jargon, a kind of magical expression akin to what Walter Benjamin had called an "aura." The words themselves became, like the cult of advertisement that was also under critique at the time, a system of signs rather than of content, pointing toward nothing but themselves. Like the fetishism of commodities, the fetishism of jargon elevated key terms—in the case of the existentialists, terms like *death, care, Man, existence,* and above all *authenticity*—to the status of (idealized, objective) things, as if they had not been shaped and formed, or deformed, by history and culture.

Adorno's description of this "cult of authenticity" is scathing. Its proponents are "anti-intellectual intellectuals."[54]

The existentialist jargon, in fact, makes the word *transcendence* what Adorno calls, with fine contempt, "the Wurlitzer organ of the spirit." Thus the particular "stereotypes of the jargon" are evidence of the opposite of what they claim: "They seem to guarantee that one is not doing what in fact he is doing—bleating with the crowd—simply by virtue of his using those stereotypes to guarantee that one has achieved it all himself." And again, "One needs only to be a believer—no matter what he believes in."[55] Adorno's critique of the philosophers is also a critique of what he calls the Pyrrhic quest for the genuine: "The genuineness of need and belief, which is questionable anyway, has to turn itself into the criterion for what is desired and believed; and in this way it becomes no longer genuine. This is the reason why no one can say the word 'genuineness' without becoming ideological."[56]

Take note of these terms: *authenticity, genuineness, transcendence, belief.* To Adorno these are the worst of jargon words, since they simulate thought and emotion. Yet to many people today these words are what they would hold up in opposition to "academic jargon," the hard words and difficult concepts of modern literary and cultural theory.

Now, suppose we juxtapose to this list, for a moment, another set of words deemed "meaningless" or worse by a celebrated midcentury critic of jargon. The critic is George Orwell, the most frequently quoted and anthologized modern writer on this question, an author praised on the flyleaf of a modern edition of one of his novels as someone who "hated intellectuals, although he was a literary critic."[57]

Orwell's targets, in his famous essay "Politics and the English Language," were pamphleteers, politicians, and, indeed, professors—although in this case they were professors of political theory and biology, not of literature. His concern about muddled writing and muddled thinking would also lead him to design a whole language system, Newspeak, for the dystopia of *1984*. But it is well to bear in mind that Orwell is not inveighing against the language of specialized research. For him the enemies are "banal statements . . . given

an appearance of profundity" and, especially in art criticism
and literary criticism, words that are "meaningless" because
they are descriptive and evaluative rather than analytic, words
like (and this is his entire list): *romantic, plastic, values, human,
dead, sentimental, natural, vitality.*

*Romantic, plastic, values, human, dead, sentimental, natural,
vitality.* If I am not mistaken, these words are the very kind
that literary critics today are scolded for *not* using. He singles
out for special scorn "the jargon words *dead* and *living*" in the
hypothetical example of a critic who writes "The outstanding
feature of Mr. X's work is its living quality" and another who
celebrates "its peculiar deadness." What he describes as "the
special connection between politics and the debasement of
language" resides in letting "ready-made phrases . . . con-
struct your sentences for you," and "even think your thoughts
for you," to the point that they may even conceal their meaning from you.[58]

So here we encounter the full extent of our fascinating
paradox, and its equally fascinating corollary:

1. The concept of jargon can be used to describe two
equal and opposite tendencies in language: the overwrought,
compact, and highly technical (or "foreign"), and the overly
familiar, flabby, and banal. These are two radically opposing
forms. We are most familiar, these days, with the first tendency, but Locke, Orwell, and Adorno also use the word *jargon* to describe the empty, fraudulent, "passing" language of
the majority culture.

2. Jargon is *any* kind of language that has been overused
and now substitutes for thought, a mere container for think-

ing, a verbal gesture rather than an idea, whether highly technical or highly banal.

3. If these two equal and opposite tendencies, which are critiques of one another, are both valid, and I think they are, then taking this idea to its furthest point, a neologism is the only kind of word that *isn't* jargon, because it has been invented to suit the particularity of the moment and the needs of thought.

4. But neologisms (new words, coinages, portmanteau words) are precisely what are labeled and excoriated as jargon.

5. So *no* words can escape this damning label. They are *all* jargon, all terms of art.

It is tempting to close on this paradoxical note of linguistic impossibility.

But I would like, instead, to offer another, much more optimistic kind of reading of the story of jargon, one that takes as its ground not the impossibility of language but its intrinsic doubleness. And for this I will have to return, for a few moments, to an unlikely and unwitting champion for literary theory, George Orwell.

Double Talk

It would be interesting to know what kind of response Orwell might have had to the movement that has grown up in his name. In 1972 the National Council of Teachers of English established a Committee on Public Doublespeak, which began awarding its first Doublespeak Award in 1974. That year it also began to publish the *Quarterly Review of Doublespeak.*

In subsequent years, there have appeared books with the following Orwell-inspired titles:

- *Double-speak in America* (1973)
- *Teaching about Doublespeak* (1976)
- *Doublespeak Dictionary* (1979)
- *Doublespeak, from "Revenue Enhancement" to "Terminal Living": How Government, Business, Advertisers and Others Use Language to Deceive You* (1981)
- *The Modern Newspeak* (1984)
- *Beyond Nineteen Eighty-Four: Doublespeak in a Post-Orwellian Age* (1989)
- *The New Doublespeak: Why No One Knows What Anyone's Saying Anymore* (1996)[59]

The target of most of these volumes is public language, the bloated vocabulary and syntax of government, business, advertising, bureaucracy, and politics. All but one of them, incidentally, concern *American* speech and writing. And all of them are takeoffs on Orwell's brilliant satirical invention, the language he called Newspeak, whose principles are articulated in an appendix to *1984.*

But as so often happens with imitations and takeoffs, the "doublespeak" industry has, to a certain extent, misspoken when it comes to citing Orwell. For a closer glance at the "Principles of Newspeak" makes it clear that the goal was the *reduction* of language's potential, not its proliferation and expansion—in short, the *elimination* of doubleness. New-

speak's A vocabulary ("words needed for the business of everyday life," purged of "all ambiguities and shades of meaning"), its B vocabulary ("words which had been deliberately
constructed for political purposes"), and its C vocabulary of
scientific and technical terms were all intended to control
language, "by eliminating undesirable words and by stripping
such words as remained of unorthodox meanings, and so far
as possible of all secondary meanings whatever."[60]

> The greatest difficulty facing the compilers of the Newspeak
> dictionary was not to invent new words, but, having invented
> them, to make sure what they meant: to make sure, that is to
> say, what ranges of words they canceled by their existence. . . .
> The Newspeak vocabulary was tiny, and new ways of reducing
> it were constantly being devised. Newspeak, indeed, differed
> from almost all other languages in that its vocabulary grew
> smaller instead of larger ever year. Each reduction was a
> gain.[61]

Linguists have drawn a connection between the notion
that language is dangerously double and the question of jargon through their critique of what have been called "weasel-
words," a term coined in 1900 and made popular by President Theodore Roosevelt. A "weasel-word," drawing its name
from the idea that a weasel sucks all the meat out of an egg
and leaves the empty shell, is an "equivocating or ambiguous
word which deliberately takes away the force or meaning of
the concept being expressed." These equivocations were initially political hedges or quibbles ("it is alleged"; "all things
being equal"; or the original example offered by the term's
inventor, Stewart Chapin, "*duly* protected"), but the concept

had, as will be appreciated, an immediate appeal to the na-
scent industry of advertising, where it almost immediately became a term of art.[62] Thus we are offered "pre-owned," rather
than used or second-hand, cars, eggs described as "jumbo"
and olives of "colossal" size, as well as products that are "new"
and offers that are "free" only in a highly qualified sense of
those words. "I'm not a doctor, but I play one on TV," when
spoken by a familiar-looking actor wearing a white coat and
advertising an over-the-counter painkiller, is the weasel effect
in action, since the scripted disavowal is at odds with all the
visual cues.

The association of weasels and words considerably pre-
dates Theodore Roosevelt, however. And perhaps it should
not be considered, in its metaphorical use, so unambiguously
negative. "I can suck melancholy out of a song, as a weasel
sucks eggs," says the melancholic aesthete Jaques in Shakespeare's *As You Like It*, imploring a singer for another "stanzo"
of a poem.[63] Jaques is a literary critic, but not a sentimental
one. The sucking-out of melancholy—a highly desired emotion in the early modern period, one associated with art,
learning, and privilege—does not render the song worthless
or empty; the next listener can undertake another interpreta-
tion, elicit another emotional or intellectual response. So
too with textual analysis in general, and scholars, both general and particular. The ambiguity of words, their self-differ-
ence, is an aspect of their particularity, their intensity, and
their power.

Let us therefore pause for a moment to contemplate
George Orwell's actual description of "doublethink," which

has been occluded somewhat by the easy popularity of egregious examples of "doublespeak."

Here is what Orwell wrote:

> To know and not to know, to be conscious of complete truthfulness while telling carefully constructed lies, to hold simultaneously two opinions which cancelled out, knowing them to be contradictory and believing in both of them. . . . Even to understand the word "doublethink" involved the use of doublethink.

"Even to understand the word 'doublethink' involved the use of doublethink." Doublethought-through, this observation, this description of the mind getting itself around a concept that seems to question its very bases for thought, is not so clearly a picture of corruption, however Orwell may have intended it.

Shorn for a moment of our preconceptions about politics and political deception, Orwell's definition of doublethink is a very shrewd and tight description of intellectual work. Of thinking. And, indeed, of literary (and cultural) analysis. To be capable of holding two views which may well "cancel out"; to "know and not to know"; to know them to be contradictory and to believe—in nuanced ways—in both of them. Everyone can see what is wrong with duplicitousness as a character trait, but it is important to recognize that this very same capacity for seeing the intertwining and doubling of truth and falsehood is central to intellectual life, in forms like paradox, hypothesis, dialectic, revision, and that concept crucial to philosophy, the counterfactual.

Take a relatively familiar example, "literary ambiguity," a favorite tool of the old New Critics. Or indeed one of its crucial elements, the "double meaning" of words. In the early modern period, the word *die* was familiar slang for sexual climax; when a poet swore that he wanted to *die* with his mistress, especially when the context was a scene set in bed, the audience could read or hear the doubleness and the (serious) joke. This intrinsic *mistaking* is one of the things that enables poetic language to function. The cultural mistrust of such doubleness in language is clear in the ill repute of the pun, the proverbial "lowest form of humor." But—or and—poetry, puns, and jokes *are* doublethink. They make you think twice: "Come again?" They perform the intellectual equivalent of the "double take," a delayed reaction that reverses and revises an initial impression. They present the impossible as possible, and even "true."

The reputation of "literary ambiguity" has gone up and down in the world with the ascendancy and decline of New Criticism. A more recent version is "counterintuitive" thinking, a crucial element of poststructuralism, though also of the teachings of Socrates. The counterintuitive is something in a passage that contradicts our empirical, commonsensical understanding of the world and the nature of meaning, but can't be ruled out, because the logic of the text allows for it. As a result, conventional wisdom is put in question.

We are used to the operations of the counterintuitive in other realms, like science (where it has often been labeled "heresy" by opponents): consider, once again, Copernicus and Galileo and the question of whether the earth moves around the sun.[64] Counterintuition is also, apparently, acceptable and even appealing in popular culture; witness the following headline from *Newsweek* about a steak-and-butter diet: "The Trendy Diet That Sizzles: A Counterintuitive Program Reaches Critical Mass."[65] In criticism, however, the counterintuitive has been more suspect. Derrida claims that writing is prior to speech; Butler asserts that "the inner truth of gender is a fabrication."[66] Each is ridiculed—in certain quarters—for going against common sense. Just look at a toddler, say their critics: a baby talks before it writes; a child "knows" the difference between male and female. Empirical evidence of this "commonsensical" kind is considered damning against the philosophical counterintuitive. "The sun moves; the earth is flat: I can see it with my own eyes."

And here is where counterintuition, or ambiguity, or any other sign of doubled and split consciousness and language, intersects with jargon. Jargon marks the place where thinking has been. It becomes a kind of macro, to use a computer term: a way of storing a complicated sequence of thinking operations under a unique name. This is true both for ideas widely shared and for counterintuitive formulations like those of literary theorists. The energy that once went into its design, its act of thinking, is represented only by a sign. By a word. By a vocabulary. The presence of a sign does not prevent, but also does not guarantee, the presence of a thought.

As we have seen, when the thought is a borrowed thought rather than one infused with the energy of thinking, a thought iterated or parroted rather than fully understood, the effect can be that of the ventriloquist rather than the speaker. This can be as true of the platitudes of "virtue" as of the polysyllables of "discourse." But it is not the fault of the *words*: to cite Adorno once again, in a slightly different context "the blame is misdirected."

"'Jargon' is not an instrument of appearances," wrote Roland Barthes, "'Jargon' is a way of imagining (and shocks as imagination does), a way of approaching metaphorical language which intellectual discourse will need one day."[67] We may recall that Adorno thought "shock" was "the only way to reach human beings through language." What Brecht called *defamiliarization* (often translated as "alienation") and what the Russian Formalist critics called the device of "deformation or *estrangement*"[68] are other versions of this salutary shock, of which jargon (for example, words like *defamiliarization* and *estrangement*) is a highly useful tool. In fact, in a world made up of and by language, we cannot do without it.

Jargon *is* language, language that shows the stresses and cracks of ideas in process and in practice. Too stale; too new. Too foreign; too familiar. Too pedantic; too demotic. Too plain; too fancy. With all these contradictory strikes against it, clearly jargon must be doing something right. Without it we speak and read a dead language, language as a museum or a shrine. It's fighting about it that keeps it alive.

Since language is transformative, seeking to engage with and bring into being thoughts and concepts, it is *neither* the moment of discovering supposed "jargon" *nor* the moment of discovering supposed "clarity" or resistance to jargon that should stand, for us, as its crowning achievement. This is a *dialectical process,* moving back and forth: it is pointless merely to "defend' jargon or to "attack" it—or, if not pointless, it is beside the point. For that sequence of "defense" and "attack," which has, as we have seen, a long history, is the record of repeated and necessary attempts to keep language from stalling in its tracks. We need—language needs, human beings need—both steps, or both sets of steps; the terms and their critique. The critique of terms that seem to presuppose insiders and outsiders, as well as the critique of language that presents itself as fully present and transparent, as having "no agenda." Every utterance, every word, has "an agenda" in this sense: remember that *agenda* is a word (derived from the Latin for "action") that means "things to do."

The philosopher J. L. Austin, the author of *How to Do Things with Words,* used the word *infelicity* to describe a kind of speech act that misfires, misinvokes, misexecutes, or abuses. Hamlet, perhaps the greatest wordsmith in English, enjoined the too-correct Horatio, on his deathbed, to "absent" himself "from felicity awhile / To tell my story." The infelicitous lies on the path to felicity.

"I, too, dislike it," wrote poet Marianne Moore about poetry. It is also an easy thing to say about jargon. In a longer draft of her poem, Moore expanded the sentiment, observing that when things "become so derivative as to become unintelligible, the same thing can be said for all of us, that we do not admire what we cannot understand."[69] But in its final version the poem read simply this way:

> I, too, dislike it.
>> Reading it, however, with a perfect contempt for it, one
>> discovers in it, after all, a place for the genuine.

It seems fitting that this poem should come to rest on the word *genuine*, a word which, as we have seen in discussions of jargon, always raises the question of its own meaning.

For those who care about words, about expression, about that which thinks *through* language, the history of jargon is the history of ideas in the making, the history of how the infelicitous becomes felicitous, and vice versa, the history of language, of hard ideas as well as hard words—the history, in short, of our terms of art.

NOTES

Chapter 1
The Amateur Professional and the Professional Amateur

1. Peter Applebome, "Check Out the 'Me, Reborn' Generation," *New York Times*, November 22, 1998, sec. 4, p. 1.

2. Quoted in Gail Collins, "A Knick Reborn," *New York Times*, November 16, 1999, A31.

3. Tony Collins, "Two Very Different Nations at Play," *Independent* (London), July 18, 1998, Obituary section, 7.

4. Amy Rosewater, "Skating Rules Hard to Figure: Difference between Pro and Amateur Is Blurred," *Plain Dealer*, October 29, 1998, 1D.

5. *Encyclopedia Britannica*, 15th ed., s.v. "Olympic Games."

6. Debbie Schlussel, "College Athletics Are Not for Amateurs," *Detroit News*, November 6, 1998, A19. Michael Hiestand, "CBS Locks In College Hoops for $454M," *USA Today*, November 19, 1999, C1.

7. Renaissance scholar Marjorie Hope Nicolson wrote of the passion that detective stories stir in professors: "Often the detective is not a professional . . . or at least not one connected with one of the central bureaus here or abroad." But the "connoisseur of detective stories," like every other expert, "despises the amateur" and wants

only to talk detection with others equally up on the genre. Nicolson, "The Professor and the Detective" (1929), in Howard Haycraft, ed., *The Art of the Mystery Story* (New York: Carroll and Graf, 1974), 117, 119.

8. Sir Arthur Conan Doyle, "The 'Gloria Scott,' " in *The Memoirs of Sherlock Holmes* (New York: Berkeley, 1963), 77–78.

9. In fact, as Nicolson points out, detectives, like scholars, follow one of only two investigative methods: the Baconian accumulation of details or the Descartian method of "intuition."

10. Henry Peacham, *Peacham's Compleat Gentleman* (1634), ed. G. S. Gordon (Oxford: Clarendon, 1906), 104–5, cited in Walter S. Houghton, Jr., "The English Virtuosi in the Seventeenth Century," *Journal of the History of Ideas* 3.1 (1942): 52. Houghton, 58, 63. Mark Girouard, *Life in the English Country House* (New Haven: Yale University Press, 1978), 165, 172.

11. Walter S. Houghton, Jr., "The English Virtuosi in the Seventeenth Century." *Journal of the History of Ideas* 3.1 (January 1942): 55.

12. Matthew Arnold, *Cornhill Magazine* 13 (1866): 290. Mark Pattison, *Suggestions on Academical Organisation with Especial Reference to Oxford* (Edinburg: Edmonston and Douglas, 1868), 293; John Middleton Murry, "What Is Style?" in *Pencillings: Little Essays on Literature* (London: W. Collins and Co., 1923), 108.

13. Herbert Muschamp, "The Passages of Paris and of Benjamin's Mind," *New York Times*, January 16, 2000, sec. 2, p. 1.

14. David Walton, "Boy Toys of Belles-Lettres," *Star Tribune* (Minneapolis), December 5, 1999, 9F.

15. Timothy P. Duffy, "The Gender of Letters: Charles Eliot Norton and the Decline of the Amateur Intellectual Tradition," *New England Quarterly* 69.1 (1996): 91–109. The following discussion of Norton is greatly indebted to Duffy's essay.

16. The quoted passage comes from the bequest of by C. C. Stillman (Harvard class of 1898) in 1925, which established the Charles Eliot Norton Professorship of Poetry.

17. *Letters of Charles Eliot Norton*, ed. Sara Norton and M. A. Dewolfe Howe, 2 vols. (Boston: Houghton Mifflin, 1913), 2:77, cited in Duffy.

18. Norton, "Feminine Poetry," *Nation*, February 24, 1876, 133. Norton, *Letters*, 1:330, cited in Duffy.

19. Duffy, 108–9.

20. Norton, *Letters*, 2:77, cited in Duffy.

21. See Burton J. Bledstein, *The Culture of Professionalism* (New York: W.W. Norton, 1976), 31.

22. "They evaded or at least mitigated just those restrictions imposed by pastoral and domestic duties which they celebrated in print; in disseminating praises of the private virtues, they gained access to the public realm." Ann Douglas, *The Feminization of American Culture* (New York: Avon, 1977), 100.

23. Robert L. Chapman, *New Dictionary of American Slang* (New York: Harper and Row, 1986), 338.

24. Thomas Bender, "Public Intellectual: Kazin: Debate about Topics That Matter," *Los Angeles Times*, June 14, 1998, M1.

25. Vivian Gornick comments on what she calls the "misogynist underside to the espoused liberal humanism" of the group. "The contempt they all felt for the idea of women as intellectual equals was visceral. Norman Mailer, Howe, Bellow—every one of them turned pathologic, hissing and spitting at the feminists." Vivian Gornick, "Alfred Kazin: The Good Enemy," *Los Angeles Times Book Review*, June 14, 1998, 4.

26. Sylvia Nasar, "New Breed of College All-Star: Columbia Pays Top Dollar for Economics Heavy Hitter," *New York Times*, April 8, 1998, D1. Sylvia Nasar, "Economics All-Star Says He Will Stay with Home Team, after All," *New York Times*, April 14, 1998, D1. The

newspaper article that began with "Speaking fees. Are they academia's dirty little secret?" went on to lay out the issues: "Instead of a pure pursuit of scholarly inquiry, the argument goes, big-fee speakers are cynically cashing in on their campus-based fame." Anthony Flint, "On Campus," *Boston Globe*, November 21, 1993, 83. Glenn Altshuler and Isaac Kramnick, "Endowing the Rich and Famous: Celebrity Speakers on Campuses," *Chronicle of Higher Education*, August 14, 1998, A48.

27. Quoted in Tom Scocca, "Going Public," *Lingua Franca*, March 1999, 9.

28. Carlin Romano, "The Dirty Little Secret about Publicity Intellectuals," *Chronicle of Higher Education*, February 19, 1999, B4.

29. Diego Ribandeneira, "From Cloister to Celebrity: Nun Artfully Bears Cross of Critic's Fame,"*Boston Globe*, December 5, 1998, B2.

30. Rebecca Pepper Sinkler, "My Case of Oprah Envy: She's Got America Reading—and Critics Weeping,"*Washington Post*, April 6, 1997, C1. Stephen Braun, "The Oprah Seal of Approval," *Los Angeles Times*, March 9, 1997, Calendar section, 8.

31. Nell Baldwin, executive director of the National Book Foundation, quoted in Bob Minzesheimer, "Winfrey's Book Talk Wins Publishing Gold," *USA Today*, November 17, 1999, D1.

32. [William Whewell], "*The Connection of the Sciences* by Mrs. Somerville," *Quarterly Review* 101 (1834): 59. See also Sydney Ross, "Scientist: The Story of a Word," *Annals of Science* 18 (1962): 65–85, where it is suggested that Whewell himself was "the ingenious gentleman."

33. Snow used the term in "The Two Cultures," *New Statesman*, October 6, 1956. It then became the title of his famous Rede Lecture in 1959 and the subsequently published book.

34. Lionel Trilling, "The Leavis-Snow Controversy," reprinted in *Beyond Culture: Essays on Literature and Learning* (New York: Viking, 1965), 152.

35. William Whewell, *The Philosophy of the Inductive Sciences: Founded upon Their History* (London: J. W. Parker, 1840), 2:230. E. O. Wilson, interview with Jeremy Manier, *Chicago Tribune*, June 14, 1998, Perspective section, 3.

36. Robert C. Berwick, "All Together Now," *Los Angeles Times*, August 30, 1998, Book Review section, 12. Michael Pakenham, "Edward O. Wilson's 'Consilience'—A Heroic Call to Make Knowledge Coherent," *Sun* (Baltimore), March 22, 1998, 4F.

37. David Warren, "Consilience, Yin and Yang," *Ottawa Citizen*, May 17, 1998, D15.

38. Tzvetan Todorov, "The Surrender to Nature," *New Republic*, April 27, 1998, 29–33.

39. Carl Djerassi, "Lastword: The Questionnaire," *Guardian*, August 8, 1998, 54.

40. Robert Strauss, "Cyberculture: Dramatic Discovery: Chemist-Turned-Author Uses Writing to Explore the Social Impacts of Pioneering Science," *Los Angeles Times*, January 12, 1998, D3.

41. Strauss, p. D3.

42. David L. Chandler, "Electromagnetic Link to TWA 800 Studied," *Boston Globe*, July 14, 1998, A10.

43. "Nation in Brief: EMI Might Have Downed Plane," *Atlanta Constitution*, July 13, 1998, 4A.

44. "Harvard Professor's Theory on Flight 800," *San Francisco Chronicle*, July 13, 1998, A5.

45. James Glanz, "Steven Weinberg: Physicist Ponders God, Truth, and 'Final Theory,' " *New York Times*, January 25, 2000, F1. There were times, of course, when literary criticism and theory *did* attempt to reach the status of a science, as in the work of linguist

Roman Jakobson. But even in those days no prize for "poet as scientist" was in the offing.

46. For Snow, of course, the opposing cultures were "literary intellectuals" and "physical scientists." C. P. Snow, *The Two Cultures* (Cambridge: Cambridge University Press, 1993), 4.

47. "What's the (Next) Big Idea?" *Inside the New York Times* 3.1 (1999). *INYT* is "A Newsletter Exclusively for New York Times Home Delivery Subscribers."

48. Dinitia Smith, "Philosopher Gamely in Defense of His Ideas," *New York Times*, May 30, 1998, B7.

49. Dinitia Smith, " 'Queer Theory' Is Entering the Literary Mainstream," *New York Times*, January 17, 1998, B9.

50. Jesse McKinley, "For the High-Minded, It's Blah, Blah, Blah: Talks Are Cheap for Seekers of Ideas Who Are Willing to Listen," *New York Times*, June 26, 1999, B9.

51. Sarah Boxer, "I Shop, Ergo I Am," *New York Times*, March 28, 1998, B7. Dinitia Smith, "With the Apocalypse Almost Now, It Becomes a New Field of Study," *New York Times*, November 8, 1997, B11.

52. Peter Edidin and Jeffrey Kittay, "Letter to Our Readers," *Lingua Franca*, premier issue (1990): 2.

53. Jeffrey Kittay and Peter Edidin, quoted in Susann Brenna, "Literary Magazine Has Its Eye on Humanities," *Newsday*, January 16, 1991, sec. 2, p. 48.

54. David Yaffe, "Fascinating Rhythm," *Lingua Franca*, October 1998, 13.

55. Paula Span, "Lingua Franca, the magazine of Naked Academia," *Washington Post*, May 25, 1993, B1.

56. Gordon N. Ray, *Professional Standards and American Editions: A Response to Edmund Wilson* (New York: Modern Language Association, 1969), i.

57. Jon Wiener, "The Footnote Fetish," *Telos* 31 (1977): 174–75.

58. Gertrude Himmelfarb, "Where Have All the Footnotes Gone?" *New York Times Book Review,* June 16, 1991. Reprinted in Himmelfarb, *On Looking into the Abyss: Untimely Thoughts on Culture and Society* (New York: Knopf, 1994).

59. Mel Gussow, "A Prospero or a Lear? Nay, Verily a Falstaff," *New York Times,* November 16, 1998, sec. E, p. 1.

60. Gussow, 1ff.

61. Harold Bloom, *The Anxiety of Influence: A Theory of Poetry* (London: Oxford University Press, 1973), 14–16.

62. Jerome McGann, "Formalism, Savagery, and Care: The Function of Criticism Once Again," *Critical Inquiry* 2.3 (1976): 629.

63. Elizabeth W. Bruss, *Beautiful Theories* (Baltimore and London: Johns Hopkins University Press, 1982), 285.

64. Bruss, 217.

65. Bruss, 285.

66. Harold Bloom, *The Flight to Lucifer: A Gnostic Fantasy* (New York: Farrar, Strauss and Giroux, 1976).

67. Quotes from professors Emory Elliott and Anne A. Cheng, in Scott Heller, "Wearying of Cultural Studies, Some Scholars Rediscover Beauty," *Chronicle of Higher Education,* December 4, 1998, A15–16.

68. Edward Rothstein, "An Amateur's Love Might Cure the Common Cough," *New York Times,* January 18, 1999, B2.

69. The scene in question is described in Wayne Booth, *For the Love of It: Amateuring and Its Rivals* (Chicago: University of Chicago Press, 1999), 61.

70. Wendy Lesser, *The Amateur: An Independent Life of Letters* (New York: Pantheon, 1999), 5.

71. James Shapiro, "The Passionate Observer," *New York Times Book Review,* February 28, 1999, 12.

72. R. P. Blackmur, "A Critic's Job of Work," in Hazard Adams, *Critical Theory since Plato*, rev. ed. (Fort Worth, Tex.: Harcourt Brace Jovanovich, 1992), 885.

73. The original charter had discouraged the taking of a higher degree. "A Junior Fellow is not allowed to be a candidate for a degree. The founders of the Society had in mind particularly the degree of Doctor of Philosophy. They felt that the Ph.D. degree, with its high but rigid standards, and its thorough but routine apprenticeship, provided a good training for many scholars, but that its atmosphere was not always best for the man who was capable of doing independent research and had an idea of his own that he wanted to follow out to the end." From George C. Homans and Orville T. Bailey, "The Society of Fellows, Harvard University, 1933–1947," in Crane Brinton, ed., *The Society of Fellows* (Cambridge: Harvard University Press, 1959), 34. The rules as of 1959 (which still described all prospective Fellows as "men") permitted Fellows to write their Ph.D. theses and take exams pursuant to the degree during the time of their incumbency, and indeed to count two full academic years as a Junior Fellow "as fulfilling the minimum residence requirements for the Harvard doctorate." Brinton, p. 71.

74. Adams, p. 884.

75. Immanuel Kant, *The Critique of Judgement*, trans. James Creed Meredith (Oxford: Clarendon, 1952), 41–89.

CHAPTER 2
DISCIPLINE ENVY

1. First line of the song "High Diddle-Dee-Dee," words by Ned Washington, music by Leigh Harline, from *Pinocchio* (Burbank, Calif.: Walt Disney, 1940).

2. Sigmund Freud, *Group Psychology and the Analysis of the Ego* (1921), in *The Standard Edition of the Complete Psychological Works of Sigmund Freud*, ed. James Strachey (London: Hogarth Press and the Institute of Psycho-Analysis, 1986), 18:101. The actual phrase "the narcissism of minor differences" appears not in this essay but in *Civilization and Its Discontents* (1930), *SE* 21:114.

3. John Dewey, "History of Education" (1907), in *The Later Works*, ed. Jo Ann Boydston (Carbondale, Ill.: 1990), 17: 183–84.

4. F.C.S. Schiller, "From Plato to Protagoras," in *Studies in Humanism* (London, 1907), 31.

5. Guy Cromwell Field, "Sophists," *The Oxford Classical Dictionary*, ed. N.G.L. Hammond and H. H. Scullard, 2d ed. (Oxford: Clarendon, 1970), 1000.

6. Derrida, "Plato's Pharmacy," in *Dissemination*, trans. Barbara Johnson (Chicago: University of Chicago Press, 1981), 108. Søren Kierkegaard, *The Concept of Irony: With Constant Reference to Socrates*, trans. Lee M. Capel (Bloomington: Indiana University Press, 1989).

7. Lewis Carroll, *The Annotated Alice*, ed. with intro. and notes by Martin Gardner (New York: New American Library, 1960), 93–94,102.

8. In a prose poem by Baudelaire, life is imagined as a hospital in which each sick person longs to be in a different bed. "Cette vie est un hôpital où chaque malade est possédé du désir de changer de lit." Charles Baudelaire, *Le Spleen de Paris*, ch. 48, in *Oeuvres complètes* (Paris: Gallimard, 1975), 356.

9. Thorstein Veblen, *The Theory of the Leisure Class* (1899; New York: Modern Library, 1934), 25.

10. *Oxford English Dictionary*, s.v. "jealousy," 4b. *Oxford English Dictionary*, s.v. "envy" 4a, b; 5.

11. René Girard, *A Theater of Envy: William Shakespeare* (New York: Oxford University Press, 1991), 4.

12. Richard Dawkins, *The Selfish Gene* (1976; Oxford and New York: Oxford University Press, 1989), 4–5, 267.

13. Philip Sidney, *Defence of Poesy* (1595), ed. Dorothy M. Macardle (London: Macmillan, 1962), 12–14.

14. Johann Wolfgang van Goethe, letter to Johann Peter Eckermann, March 23, 1829. Friedrich von Schelling, *Philosophie der Kunst,* 576.

15. Walter Pater, "The School of Giorgione," in *The Renaissance* (1877) (New York: Meridian Books, 1961), 132.

16. Oscar Wilde, "The Decay of Lying," in *The Complete Works of Oscar Wilde,* intro. Vyvyan Holland (New York: Harper and Row, 1989), 987.

17. They are: Jerome Friedman, Walter Gilbert, Sheldon Glashow, Dudley Herschbach, Edwin Krebs, William Lipscomb, Richard Roberts, Mel Schwartz.

18. Vinay L. Kashyap, of Harvard-Smithsonian Center for Astrophysics, "mini-AIR" (March 1997), the on-line monthly supplement to *Annals of Improbable Research,* at <www.improbable. com/airchives/miniair/twentieth-century/MINI9703>

19. Victoria E. Bonnell and Lynn Hunt, eds., *Beyond the Cultural Turn* (Berkeley: University of California Press, 1999). See especially the preface and introduction. See also Geoff Eley, "Is All the World a Text? From Social History to the History of Society Two Decades Later," in Terrence J. McDonald, *The Historic Turn in the Human Sciences* (Ann Arbor: University of Michigan Press, 1996), 193–244.

20. Melanie Klein, "Envy and Gratitude" (1957), in *Envy and Gratitude and Other Works, 1946–1963* (New York: Delacorte, 1975), 178–79.

21. Irene Fast, "Developments in Gender Identity," in Nancy Burke, ed., *Gender and Envy* (New York and London: Routledge, 1999), 162.

22. Hanna Segal, *Introduction to the Works of Melanie Klein* (New York: Basic Books, 1974), 40.

23. Segal, 45.

24. Jessica Benjamin, *The Bonds of Love* (New York: Pantheon, 1988), 111.

25. Søren Kierkegaard, *The Sickness Unto Death*, trans. Walter Lowrie (Princeton: Princeton University Press, 1946), 139.

26. Maureen Dowd, "Streetcar Named Betrayal," *New York Times*, February 24, 1999, A23.

27. Ann Douglas, *The Feminization of American Culture* (New York: Avon, 1977), 123.

28. Elizabeth Haiken, *Venus Envy: A History of Cosmetic Surgery* (Baltimore: Johns Hopkins University Press, 1997); Adam Mars-Jones, *Venus Envy* (London: Chatto and Windus, 1990); Rita Mae Brown, *Venus Envy* (New York: Bantam, 1993).

29. Kevin Kopelson, *Beethoven's Kiss: Pianism, Perversion, and the Mastery of Desire* (Stanford: Stanford University Press, 1996).

30. David Firestone, "In Television News, an Epidemic of Pencil Envy," *New York Times,* January 10, 1999, sec. 4, p. 6.

31. Alan Sokal, "Transgressing the Boundaries: Toward a Transformative Hermeneutics of Quantum Gravity," *Social Text* 46/47 (spring/summer 1996): 217–52.

32. Edward Rothstein, "Ideas & Trends: When Wry Hits Your Pi From a Real Sneaky Guy," *New York Times*, May 26, 1996, sec. 4, p. 6.

33. Alan Sokal and Jean Bricmont, *Fashionable Nonsense: Postmodern Intellectuals' Abuse of Science* (New York: Picador, 1998), 5.

34. Roland Barthes, "Research: The Young," in *The Rustle of Language*, trans. Richard Howard (Berkeley and Los Angeles: University of California Press, 1989), 72.

35. Stanley Fish, "Being Interdisciplinary Is So Very Hard to Do," *Profession* 89, 15–22.

36. Vendler reminded her audience of an earlier, paradisal moment, invoking "that early attitude of entire receptivity and plasticity and innocence before the text . . . before we knew what research libraries or variorum editions were, before we had heard any critical terms, before we had seen a text with footnotes." Helen Vendler, "Presidential Address 1980," *PMLA* 96.3 (1981): 344–48.

37. Edward Said, "Restoring Intellectual Coherence," *MLA Newsletter*, spring 1999, 3.

38. "Most medical schools now have a bioethics and humanities curriculum. Many have full medical humanities departments . . . interestingly, many schools have found that the study of literature is a remarkable way to restore humanism in medicine. Students witness much carnage in a hospital, and medical training often promotes a certain machismo that discourages them from expressing emotion. I find that by reading and discussing *The Death of Ivan Ilyich*, for example, or William Carlos Williams's "The Use of Force," or Ralph Ellison's *Invisible Man*, senior students who are at first reluctant to engage in such nonscientific pursuits often have a catharsis of sorts, which brings insight into their patients' situations as well as their own." Abraham Verghese, "Showing Doctors Their Biases," *New York Times*, March 1, 1999, A25. "Scholars doing what's been called 'the new Jewish studies' can find themselves between two worlds—seen as 'too Jewish' for the humanities, but not suited for traditional Jewish-studies programs, which have stressed expertise in biblical literature and history." Scott Heller, "The New Jewish Studies: Defying Tradition and Easy Categorization," *Chronicle of Higher Education*, January 29, 1999, A21.

39. Gabriel Schoenfeld, "Death Camps as Kitsch," *New York Times*, March 16, 1999, A25.

40. On the disciplinary establishment of American studies, see Ellen Rooney, "Discipline and Vanish," *differences: A Journal of Feminist Cultural Studies* 2.5 (1990): 17–28; Gene Wise, " 'Paradigm Dra-

mas' in American Studies: A Cultural and Institutional History of the Movement," *American Quarterly* 32 (1979): 293–337; and Michael Denning, " 'The Special American Conditions': Marxism and American Studies," *American Quarterly* 38 (1986): 356–80.

41. Janny Scott, "MacArthur 'Genius' Grants Get Some Heat and a New Head," *New York Times*, December 9, 1997, G5. John Leo, "How to Be a Rich Genius," *U.S. News & World Report*, June 26, 1995, 24.

42. "Native intellectual power of an exalted type, such as is attributed to those who are esteemed greatest in any department of art, speculation, or practice; instinctive and extraordinary capacity for imaginative creation, original thought, invention, or discovery. Often contrasted with *talent.*" *Oxford English Dictionary*, s.v. "genius," sense 5.

43. Jonathan Bate, *The Genius of Shakespeare* (New York: Oxford University Press, 1998), 163. Notice that it is especially fantasy, and not history, that makes Shakespeare unique, the creation of supernatural figures like ghosts, fairies, and witches: his "noble Extravagance of Fancy . . . made him capable of succeeding, where he had nothing to support him besides the Strength of his Genius." (Joseph Addison in *Spectator* 419, ed. Donald F. Bond (Oxford: Clarendon, 1965), 2:126–27.

44. Addison, *Spectator* 160, in Bond, 3:572–73.

45. "*Originals* can arise from genius only," wrote Young. "Learning we thank, Genius we revere; That gives us pleasure, This gives us rapture; That informs, This inspires; and is itself inspired, for genius is from heaven, learning from man." Young, *Conjectures on Original Composition* (1759; Leeds, England: Scolar Press, 1966), 36–37).

46. Immanuel Kant, *Critique of Judgement*, trans. J. H. Bernard (London and New York: Collier Macmillan, 1951), 150.

47. "We can readily learn all that Newton has set forth in his immortal work on the *Principles of Natural Philosophy*, however great a head was required to discover it, but we cannot learn to write spirited poetry, however express may be the precepts of the art and however excellent its models. The reason is that Newton could make all his steps, from the first elements of geometry to his own great and profound discoveries, intuitively plain and definite as regards consequence, not only to himself but to everyone else. But a Homer or a Wieland cannot show how his ideas, so rich in fancy and yet so full of thought, come together in his head, simply because he does not know and therefore cannot teach others. In science, then, the greatest discoverer only differs in degree from his laborious imitator and pupil, but he differs specifically from him whom nature has gifted for beautiful art." Kant, 151–52.

48. Kant, 153.

49. Kant, 161. The genius, by providing an example, can produce "for other good heads a school, i.e., a methodical system of teaching according to rules," but the imitator should not merely "ape" the genius in an ostentatious or pretentious manner: the pretense of genius through this kind of emulation is "like the behavior of a man of whom we say that he hears himself talk, or who stands and moves about as if he were on a stage in order to be stared at; this always betrays a bungler." Kant, 162–63.

50. Or the *OED* either; see "genius," sense 4: "Natural ability or capacity; the special endowments which fit a man for his peculiar work."

51. James Gleick, *Genius: The Life and Science of Richard Feynman* (New York: Vintage, 1992), 313. In some ways genius is out of fashion, under suspicion, indeed under erasure. Gleick notes that "in the domains of criticism that fell under the spell of structuralism and then deconstructionism," even an "unmagical" view of genius

"became suspect." (His invocation of the "spell" here is not without interest; are deconstructors and other literary theorists themselves wizards or "geniuses" in the old sense, enchanting away received truths?) To ask about genius was "to ask the wrong question." Genius is instead regarded among some scholars of literature, art, and music as "an artifact of a culture's psychology, a symptom of a particular form of hero worship." After all, "reputations of greatness come and go," conditioned to a certain extent by "sociopolitical needs" and "historical context." Whether Gleick himself concurs with this demystification of "the genius" as a kind of person is not wholly clear. What is clear, however, is that he notes the irony of the concept's migration from the time of Kant: "How strange . . . that coolly rational scientists should be the last serious scholars to believe not just in genius but in geniuses; to maintain a mental pantheon of heroes; and to bow . . . before the magicians." Gleick, 322–23.

52. Gertrude Stein, *The Autobiography of Alice B. Toklas* (1933; New York: Vintage, 1990), 87, 114.

53. Robert McAlmon, *Being Geniuses Together* (1920–30, rev. 1938 by Kay Boyle; Baltimore: Johns Hopkins University Press, 1997).

54. "The three geniuses of whom I wish to speak," writes Stein in the voice of Toklas, "are Gertrude Stein, Pablo Picasso, and Alfred Whitehead. . . . I have only known three first class geniuses and in each case on sight within me something rang." Stein, 5. That Stein believed so strongly in the existence of genius—she once said that the Jews had produced "only three originative geniuses—Christ, Spinoza, and myself"—is a sign of both its idealization and its endangerment. McAlmon, 228.

55. Virginia Woolf, *To the Lighthouse* (1927; New York: Harcourt, Brace and World, 1955), 53–55.

56. Jean-Paul Sartre, *Nausea*, trans. Lloyd Alexander (New York: New Directions, 1964), 30.

57. Arthur Conan Doyle, "The Red-headed League," in *Sherlock Holmes: The Complete Novels and Stories 1* (New York: Bantam, 1986), 1:238.

58. George Eliot, *Middlemarch* (1871–72; Middlesex, England: Penquin, 1965; Penguin Classics, 1985). The artist Will Ladislaw points out that since Casaubon doesn't know German and isn't trained as an Orientalist his work is useless and obsolete before he begins to write it up. "The subject Mr. Casaubon has chosen is as changing as chemistry; new discoveries are constantly making new points of view. Who wants a system on the basis of the four elements, or a book to refute Paracelsus? Do you not see that it is no use now to be crawling a little way after men of the last century . . . and correcting their mistakes?—living in a lumber-room. . . ." (164–65). Even his young wife, Dorothea, begins to wonder if he will ever write a word, although she wants nothing more than to be handmaiden to genius ("she felt sure that she would have accepted the judicious Hooker, if she had been born in time to save him from the wretched mistake he made in matrimony; or John Milton when his blindness had come on; or any of the other great men whose odd habits it would have been glorious piety to endure. . . . The really delightful marriage must be that where your husband was a sort of father, and could teach you even Hebrew, if you wished it" [32]).

59. The amazingly well-named Dr. Minor, a prodigious collector of books, is the one figure I know of who seems to have literalized the question of penis envy, when, in a fit of religious self-loathing, he cut off his own penis with a knife he had been allowed to possess in order to open the unfinished pages of first editions. "For both men," Winchester writes of the encounter of the two doctors, lexi-

cographer James Murray and mental patient Minor, "the first sight of the other must have been peculiar indeed, for they were uncannily similar in appearance." Both were tall, thin, and bald, with "deeply hooded blue eyes," and strikingly similar "white, long, and nicely swallow-tailed" beards. The twenty-year friendship that grew from this encounter was based "on their passionate and keenly shared love of words." Yet one was an Oxford professor and one was an autodidact—and a madman. Simon Winchester, *The Professor and the Madman* (New York: HarperCollins, 1998), 177–78.

60. Winchester, 177–78.

61. "He teaches himself," notes Roquentin. "He has read everything."

62. G. J. Warnock, *English Philosophy since 1900* (London: Oxford University Press, 1958), 172.

63. Michel Foucault, *Discipline and Punish*, trans. Alan Sheridan (New York: Vintage, 1979), 193.

64. The art-historical progress of *The School of Athens* could, if we liked, provide us with a little diagram of discipline envy. Late nineteenth-century German and English scholars seemed preoccupied with identifying every one of the fifty-six figures and what they symbolized (at least three scholars felt they had come close to doing so, though the fifty or so names each provided were by no means identical), until Wöfflin chastised them for trying to make art into history and philosophy. Wöfflin's theories of style and Panofsky's theories of iconography dominated subsequent investigations and coincided with "the institutionalization of art history as an academic discipline." (As Svetlana Alpers has observed, "to a remarkable extent the study of art and art history has been determined by the art of Italy and its study"—a narrative art of reading paintings with reference to "prior and hallowed texts" of mythology, poetry, and religion. Svetlana Alpers, *The Art of Describing: Dutch Art in the*

Seventeenth Century [Chicago: University of Chicago Press, 1983], xix–xx.) Recent scholarship on *The School of Athens*, influenced by an interest in history and visual culture, have attempted to describe the intellectual context of the papal court, through a reading of humanist theology and philosophy. Among those topics suggested as the possible subject of the painting have been "the Liberal Arts renewed by mathematical rule," *the pax philosophica* (or "the concord of Plato and Aristotle"), and the complementary nature of philosophy and theology. See Marcia B. Hall, ed., *Raphael's School of Athens* (New York: Cambridge University Press, 1997).

65. Wilhelm Dilthey, "The Dream," in William Klubach, *Wilhelm Dilthey's Philosophy of History* (New York: Columbia University Press, 1956), 103–9. Reprinted in Hans Meyerhoff, ed., *The Philosophy of History in Our Time* (Garden City, N.J.: Doubleday, 1959), 37–43. I am grateful to Geoffrey Waite for this reference.

66. Robert Maynard Hutchins, *The Great Conversation: The Substance of a Liberal Education* (Chicago: Encyclopedia Britannica, 1952). The project was the publication of *Great Books of the Western World*, a post–World War II expression of democratic intellectual optimism. Hutchins wrote in his preface to *The Great Conversation*, the volume that introduced the series, "It is the task of every generation to reassess the tradition in which it lives, to discard what it cannot use, and to bring into context with the distant and intermediate past the most recent contributions to the Great Conversation" (xi).

67. Dilthey's term of *Geisteswissenschaften*, sometimes translated as "human studies" or "human sciences," was intended to represent "the various studies of man, including history, psychology, economics, anthropology, sociology and politics." H. P. Rickman, *Wilhelm Dilthey: Pioneer of the Human Studies* (Berkeley: University of California Press, 1979), 62.

CHAPTER 3
TERMS OF ART

1. Dinitia Smith, "When Ideas Get Lost in Bad Writing," *New York Times*, February 27, 1999, A19, A21. "Academic Jargon Is a Cover," letter to the editor, *New York Times*, March 3, 1999, A22.

2. Paul Hollander, University of Massachusetts, Amherst; Timothy J. Lark, University of California, Berkeley; Leslie Peters, Gaithersburg, Maryland, letters to the editor, *New York Times*, March 3, 1999, A22.

3. Christopher Lehmann-Haupt, "Critic's Notebook: In a Glove Compartment, New Clues to 'Lear,' " *New York Times*, March 3, 1999, B1–2.

4. John Locke, *An Essay Concerning Human Understanding*, ed. Alexander Campbell Fraser (New York: Dover, 1959), 2.3.35. Matthew Prior, "I Am That I Am, an Ode" (1688) "All jargon of the schools"); Pomfret, "Love's Triumph Over Reason" (1699), ("Noisy jargon of the schools"); Cowper, "Truth" (1782) ("The sounding jargon of the schools").

5. Colet insisted that his new curriculum include "good litterature both laten and greke," as a corrective to the barbarism of the middle ages, railing against "all barbary all corrupcion all laten adulterate which ignorant blynde folis brought into this worlde," which "hath distayned and poysenyd the old laten spech and varay Romayne tong" of Cicero and Sallust and Vergil. John Colet, extract from the Statutes of St. Paul's School, in J. H. Lupton, *A Life of John Colet* (London: G. Bell and Sons, 1887), 271–84.

6. Aristotle, *Poetics*, trans., S. H. Butcher (1895; New York: Hill and Wang, 1961), 101–2.

7. Aristotle, *Poetics*, trans. Ingram Bywater (1909), in *The Complete Works of Aristotle*, Revised Oxford Translation, ed. Jonathan Barnes (Princeton: Princeton University Press, 1984), 2333.

8. Ibid.

9. "Jargon, it might be said, has become, in some modern uses, a jargon word," Raymond Williams observed some years ago. "It is now most commonly used to describe, unfavourably or contemptuously, the vocabulary of certain unfamiliar branches of knowledge or intellectual positions." In Williams's own time he found the term used in this dismissive way "mainly in relation to psychology and sociology" (he is speaking, of course, of the British kind of sociology, the forerunner of today's cultural studies) and also in relation to "an opposing intellectual position such as Marxism." Williams, a Marxist sociologist, must have got used to hearing it. "It is true," he acknowledges, "that specialized internal vocabularies can be developed, in any of these and other areas, to a fault. But it is also true that the use of a new term or the new definition of a concept is often the necessary form of a challenge to other ways of thinking or of indication of new and alternative ways. Every known general position, in matters of art and belief, has its defining terms, and the difference between these and the terms identified as jargon is often no more than one of relative date and familiarity." Raymond Williams, *Keywords* rev. ed. (New York: Oxford University Press, 1983), 175–76. Similar defenses of academic jargon have also been mounted periodically by literary scholars. See, for example, Edward Pechter, "In Defence of Jargon: Criticism as a Social Practice," *Textual Practice* 5.2 (1991), and Derek Attridge, "Arche-Jargon," *Qui Parle* 5.1 (1991): 41–52.

10. Kenneth Hudson, *The Jargon of the Professions* (London: Macmillan, 1978), 82.

11. "He was immediately captivated by the jargon and brouhaha of the sales department." Christopher Morley, *John Mistletoe* (1931), 11.95.

12. Paul Morgan and Sue Scott, *The D.C. Dialect: How to Master*

the New Language of Washington in Ten Easy Lessons (New York: Washington Mews, 1975).

13. "The Virtuecrats," Howard Fineman's cover story for *Newsweek*, June 13, 1994, 30ff., seems to have been the first public airing of this useful term. William Bennett, author of the best-selling *Book of Virtues*, is its principal subject, but the term has been used to describe politicians and other public figures, from Michael Huffington (whose emergence from the closet may have damaged his "virtue" rating with some supporters) to Dan Quayle, Ralph Reed—and Hillary Clinton.

14. Lewis Carroll, *Through the Looking-Glass*, in *The Annotated Alice*, ed. Martin Gardner (New York: New American Library, 1960), 271.

15. *Monthly Magazine* 3. 417. (*OED* neology 1). (1867; New York: Hund and Houghton, 1864), Isaac Disraeli, *Amenities of Literature* 361; Disraeli, *Curiosities of Literature* (London: G. Routledge and Co., 1858), 3:23–32.

16. Initial *OED* citations as follows: "label," *Twelfth Night*, 1.5.265; "lapse," *Cymbeline*, 3.6.12; "dialogue," *Timon of Athens*, 2.2.52; "design," *Love's Labour's Lost*, 4.1.88; "accused," *Richard II*, 1.1.17; "addiction," *Othello*, 2.2.6; "rival," *A Midsummer Night's Dream*, 4.1.139 (as adjective) and *King Lear*, 1.1.194 (as verb); "anchovy," *1 Henry IV*, 2.4.58; "grovel," *2 Henry VI*, 1.2.9; "laughable," *The Merchant of Venice*, 1.1.56; "amazement," *King John*, 5.1.35; "traditional," *Richard III*, 3.1.45; "excitement," *Hamlet*, 4.4.58; "protesters," *Julius Caesar*, 1.2.34; "circumstantial," *As You Like It*, 5.4.86; "launder," "Lover's Complaint," 16; "assassination," *Macbeth*, 1.7.2. See Jeffrey McQuain and Stanley Malless, *Coined by Shakespeare: Words and Meanings First Used by the Bard* (Springfield, Mass.: Merriam-Webster, 1998).

17. In Franz Kafka's diary (February 25, 1912), he speaks of having given "einen kleinen Einleitungsvortrag über Jargon" ("a little introductory lecture on Yiddish") *Tagebücher*, Band 2: 1912–1914,

pp. 35–36, in *Gesammelte Werke in zwölf Bänden*, ed. Hans-Gerd Koch (Frankfurt a.M.: Fischer Taschenbuch, 1994), 194. The official title of the talk is "Rede über die jiddishe Sprache," but in the talk itself Kafka consistently uses "Jargon" rather than "die jiddishe Sprache": e.g., "Der Jargon ist die jüngste europäische Sprache." (Yiddish is the most recent European language) *Hochzeitsvorbereitungen*, 421–26. In a letter to Felice Bauer, November 6, 1912, Kafka writes "Über das Jargontheater habe ich gewisse nicht ironisch gesprochen" (I certainly didn't speak ironically about the Yiddish theatre) *Briefe an Felice*, ed. Erich heller and Jürgen Born (Frankfurt a.M.: S. Fischer, 1967), 77. I am grateful to Judith Ryan for these references.

18. Samuel Taylor Coleridge, *The Rime of the Ancient Mariner*, 362. Geoffrey Chaucer, *The Merchant's Tale*, 604: "He was al coltissh ful of ragerye/And ful of Iargon as a flekked Pye." John Gower, *Confessio Amantis*, 2.264: "Sche [Medea] made many a wonder soun . . . and riht so as hir jargoun strangeth, / In sondri wise hir forme changeth."

19. *Oxford English Dictionary*, 2d ed. "jargon," sb. 3.

20. Jonathan Swift, *A Discourse of the Contests and Dissentions Between the Nobles and the Commons in Athens and Rome* (1701), ed. Frank H. Ellis (Oxford: Clarendon, 1967), 97.

21. The Summoner speaks Latin when in his cups ("a few termes hadde he, two or three, / That he had lerned out of som decree") and is compared to a parrot emptily repeating phrases he doesn't understand, while the suspect arts of Astrology ("Franklin's Tale," 538) and alchemy ("Canon's Yeoman's Prologue and Tale," 199) are the source of delightfully mystifying "termes" that make the users seem wise because their terms are "clergial" (pedantic) and "queynte." In fact the character of Chaucer in John Gay's play *The Wife of Bath* would later boast that he has memorized the twelve signs of the zodiac: "my Memory is pretty well stocked with Terms

of Art, and I can talk unintelligibly." John Gay, *The Wife of Bath* (1713), act 4, sc.1. In a play by John Dryden called *An Evening's Love; or, The Mock-Astrologer,* a young Englishman, Bellamy, tries to deceive Don Alonzo de Ribera, an old Spanish gentleman (whose daughter Bellamy would like to marry) into believing that he is an astrologer—a feat made more difficult by the fact that the Don Alonzo himself turns out to have studied astrology. Accused of not knowing the right terms, Bellamy wittily retorts, "Do not I know your Michaelmas, your Hilary, your Easter, your Trinity, and your Long Vacation terms?" placing the Spaniard, in turn, at a loss, since he finds these insider references to English school life completely mystifying. Don Alonzo protests, "I do not understand a word of this Jargon." "It may be not, Sir," says Bellamy; "I believe the terms are not the same in Spain as they are in England." "The terms of art," replies Don Alonzo sturdily, "are the same everywhere" (act 2).

22. Alison Mitchell and Don Van Natta, Jr., "G.O.P. Aide Details Tactics on Clinton," *New York Times,* October 7, 1998, A17.

23. David Mamet, *Oleanna* (New York: Vintage, 1993), 1–4.

24. Jenny Lyn Bader, "Content Provided Below," *New York Times,* August 1, 1999, sec. 4, p. 3.

25. *Listener,* November 14, 1968, 663.

26. *Times Literary Supplement,* April 6, 1973, 401.

27. Tom Kuntz, "Word for Word: Designer Babble," *New York Times,* March 28, 1999, sec. 4, p. 7.

28. Samuel Johnson, *Rambler* 163: 4, 1751; David Hume, *Essays and Treatises,* 2:134, 1776.

29. In his monumental *History of England,* Thomas Babington Macaulay wrote with passionate feeling about the "war between wit and Puritanism" in the seventeenth century and the revenge of the royalist wits against the "canting Roundhead": "To that sanctimonious jargon, which was his shibboleth, was opposed another jar-

gon not less absurd and much more odious. As he never opened his mouth except in scriptural phrase, the new breed of wits and fine gentlemen never opened their mouths without uttering ribaldry of which a porter would now be ashamed, and without calling on their Maker to curse them, sink them, confound them, blast them, and damn them." Thomas Babington Macaulay, *History of England from the Accession of James II* (Boston: Phillips, Sampson and Company, 1849), 1:313.

30. Michel Foucault, "What Is an Author?" trans. Donald F. Bouchard and Sherry Simon, in *Foucault: Language, Counter-Memory, Practice* (Ithaca: Cornell University Press, 1977), 131. Foucault, "What Is an Author?" 131–32.

31. George Steiner adumbrated four kinds of poetic difficulty, which he called *contingent* (the poem contains words you don't know but can look up), *modal* (the poem generates uncertainty about the context or mode or genre of the utterance), *tactical* (the poet is deliberately being obscure or evasive), and *ontological* (poetry puts in question the possibility of human communication through language). Of the tactically difficult poet Steiner wrote, "He will reanimate lexical and grammatical resources that have fallen out of use. He will melt and inflect words into neological shapes. He will labour to undermine, through distortion, through hyperbolic augment, through elision and displacement, the banal and constricting determinations of ordinary, public syntax." And why? "We are not meant to understand easily and quickly. Immediate purchase is denied us. . . . In certain fascinating cases our understanding, however strenuously won, is to remain provisional. There is to be an undecidability at the heart. . . . There is a dialectical strangeness in the will of the poet to be understood only step by step and up to a point." For Steiner, such difficulty is part of poetic quality. "The authentic poet cannot make do with the infinitely shop-worn inventory of speech, with the necessarily devalued,

or counterfeit currency of the every-day. He must literally create new words and syntactic modes." George Steiner, "On Difficulty," in *On Difficulty and Other Essays* (Oxford: Oxford University Press, 1978), 34–35.

32. Theodor W. Adorno, *Minima Moralia*, trans. E.F.N. Jephcott (London and New York: Verso, 1978), 101.

33. *OED* citations: *Monthly Pantheon* I.665 (1808): 1; *Academy*, August 4, 1906, 106.

34. *OED* citations: Arthur Koestler, *Invisible Writing*, 40; George Orwell, *Contemp. Jewish Record* 8:169.

35. C. S. Lewis, Letters, June 7, 1934 [1966], 157. *Nation*, May 28, 1910, 307.

36. Barbara Pym, *Quartet in Autumn*, ch. 8, p. 74. *Lancet*, May 20, 1972, 1104.

37. Maurice Isserman recalls that among young people of the so-called New Left, "it was always used in a tone mocking the pieties of our own insular political counterculture." Maurice Isserman, "Travels with Dinesh," *Tikkun* 6.5, p. 82. Among feminists in the early '80s the issue was "politically correct"—or "incorrect"—sex, where the "incorrect" included lesbianism and sadomasochism. "Political correctness," then, meant opposing practices like pornography, lesbian sexuality, and S/M, deemed exploitative by some feminists and liberating by others. "Political correctness" thus described a point of view about human sexuality presumably espoused by exactly those conservatives who today regard the phrase as a watchword of the left, and especially of so-called "radical feminists." Ruth Perry, "Historically Correct," *Women's Review of Books* 9.5 (1990).

38. As Barbara Johnson explains: "Deconstruction is not a form of textual vandalism designed to prove that meaning is impossible. In fact, the word 'de-construction' is closely related not to the word 'destruction' but to the word 'analysis,' which etymologically means

'to undo'—a virtual synonym for 'to de-construct.' " Barbara Johnson, "Translator's Introduction" to Jacques Derrida, *Dissemination*
(Chicago: University of Chicago Press, 1981), xiv–xv.

39. *Deconstruction*: "a method of analyzing texts based on the
ideas that language is inherently unstable an shifting and that the
reader rather than the author is central in determining meaning."
Deconstruct: "to subject a text to critical analysis using the theories
of deconstruction." *Encarta World English Dictionary* (New York: St.
Martin's Press, 1999), 470. Bill Johnson, letter to the editor, *Arizona
Republic*, August 12, 1999, SD6.

40. Theodor Adorno, "Words from Abroad," in *Notes to Literature*,
vol. 1, ed. Rolf Tiedemann, trans. Shierry Weber Nicholsen (New
York: Columbia University Press, 1991), 185. "Wörter aus der
Fremde," originally a talk for the Hessischer Rundfunk, was published in *Akzente* 2 (1959) 176ff. Adorno shrewdly linked this linguistic xenophobia to *Rancune* (rancor or spite, from the French)
and to *Ressentiment* ("a word currently enjoying an unfortunate popularity" that was "imported rather than invented by Nietzsche").
But he saw that, far from being a liability, the foreign word was a
useful impediment, a "Go Slow" sign on the road, an opportunity
to make the listener stop and think.

> The hard, contoured quality of the foreign word, the very thing that
> makes it stand out from the continuum of language, can be used to
> bring out what is intended but obscured by the bad generality of lan-
> guage use. Further, the discrepancy between the foreign word and
> the language can be made to serve the expression of truth. Language
> participates in reification, the separation of subject matter and
> thought. The customary ring of naturalness deceives us about that. It
> creates the illusion that what is said is immediately equivalent to what
> is meant. By acknowledging itself as a token, the foreign word re-
> minds us bluntly that all real language has something of the token in

it. It makes itself language's scapegoat, the bearer of the dissonance that language has to give form and not merely to prettify. . . . Foreign words demonstrate the impossibility of an ontology of language: they confront even concepts that try to pass themselves off as origin itself with their mediatedness, their moment of being subjectively constructed, their arbitrariness. Terminology, the quintessence of foreign words in the individual disciplines, and especially in philosophy, is not only thing-like rigidification but also its opposite: critique of concepts' claim to exist in themselves when in fact language has inscribed in them something posited, something that could be otherwise. Terminology destroys the illusion of naturalness in language. (Adorno, "Words from Abroad," 190.)

41. Theodor Adorno, *Minima Moralia* (1951), trans. E.F.N. Jephcott (London: Verso, 1978), 110.

42. Ibid., 186–87.

43. In this spirit a *New York Times* review of Alan Sokal and Jean de Bricmont's *Fashionable Nonsense*, opines mildly that "Perhaps the high-sounding verbiage has an incantatory force for those innocent of science. Some of these passages, if intoned in the plummy voice of, say, Jeremy Irons, could well have the meaningless beauty of a Mallarmé poem." Jim Holt, "Is Paris Kidding?" *New York Times*, November 15, 1998, sect. 7, p. 8.

44. Adorno, "Words from Abroad," 190.

45. Edward A. Freeman, *The History of the Norman Conquest of England* (Oxford: Clarendon Press, 1886), 5:545.

46. Cited in Isaac Disraeli, *Amenities of Literature*, 1:157.

47. Martin Cutts and Chrissie Maher, *Gobbledygook* (London: George Allen and Unwin, 1984), 7–8.

48. "Pelisse": Mrs. Delany, *Life and Corresp.* (1862). Here are some examples cited in the *OED*: "That unpalatable Ragoust, called in Latin Cramben Biscoctum, and in plain English, Twice-boil'd

Cabbage." T. Brown, *Amusem. Ser. & Com.* 10 (1700): 125. "Un ar-
rangement, which is, in plain English, a gallantry." Chesterfield,
Letters (1751), 3: 26 (no. 227). "Less efficacious": Biggs, *New Disp.*
35 (1651). Other examples: "but one twenty-fifth as useful, or in
plain English, nearly useless." Report to the Government, U.S. Mu-
nitions War (1868), 107. "A mere Rationalist (that is to say in plain
English, an Atheist)." Sanderson, Pref. Ussher's *Power Princes*
(1670).

49. Mary McCarthy, *A Charmed Life* (New York: Harcourt Brace
Jovanovich, 1955), 49. *Danziger's View.* "Down at the VFW the Susan
Faludi Fan Club Holds a Meeting," *Los Angeles Times* Syndicate, re-
printed in *Boston Globe*, September 25, 1999, A22.

50. Roland Barthes, *Criticism and Truth,* trans. Katrine Pilcher
Keuneman (Minneapolis: University of Minnesota Press, 1987), 42.

51. "You can describe this linguistic narcissism in another way:
'jargon' is the language which the Other uses; the Other (and not
Others) is that which is not yourself; this is why we find another's
way of speaking painful. As soon as a language is no longer that of
our own community we judge it to be useless, empty, raving, used
for reasons which are not serious but trivial and base (snobbery,
complacency). . . . In truth, this language is clear only to the extent
that it is generally accepted." Barthes, 49–50.

52. Barthes, 46–47.

53. Locke objects to the "artificial ignorance, and learned gibberish" of the "learned disputants, these all-knowing doctors"—
that's us, professors—who gained their authority by "amusing the
men of business, and the ignorant, with hard words, or employing
the ingenious and idle in intricate disputes about unintelligible
terms, and holding them perpetually entangled in that endless lab-
yrinth." The learned doctors are showoffs, pretentious, empty, and
fraudulent. And he finishes up with this zinger, which could—except for its particularly felicitous phrasing—be ripped from the

pages of recent diatribes against poststructuralism: "For untruth being unacceptable to the mind of man, there is no other defence left for absurdity but obscurity." John Locke, *An Essay Concerning Human Understanding*, ed. Alexander Campbell Fraser (New York: Dover, 1959), 2:123–24.

54. The jargon of authenticity, "noble and homey at once," elevated a sublanguage to a superior language, extending through the entire literate culture from departments of philosophy and theology to evening schools and youth organizations and the realms of pedagogy, business, and administration. "While the jargon overflows with the pretense of deep human emotion, it is just as standardized as the world that it officially negates." And again, "The words of the jargon sound as if they said something higher than what they mean." Theodor W. Adorno, *The Jargon of Authenticity*, trans. Knut Tarnowski and Frederic Will (Evanston, Ill.: Northwestern University Press, 1973), 4, 5, 6, 9.

55. "One can trust anyone who babbles this jargon; people wear it in their buttonholes, in place of the currently disreputable party badge. The pure tone drips with positivity, without needing to stoop too far—pleading for what is all too compromised; one escapes even the long-since-socialized suspicion of ideology." Adorno, *Jargon*, 17, 18, 21.

56. Technology—specifically the growing power of radio and television—contributed, he thought, to this false intimacy: "the voice of the announcer resounds in the home, as though he were present and knew each individual. The announcers' technically and psychologically created artificial language—the model of which is the repellently confidential 'Till we meet again'—is of the same stripe as the jargon of authenticity. The catchword for all this is *encounter*." Adorno, *Jargon*, 70, 71.

57. Biographical note to the Signet Classic edition of *1984* (New York: Penguin, 1950, 1981).

58. Orwell, "Politics," 362–65.

59. Mario Pei, *Double-Speak in America* (New York: Hawthorne Books, 1973); Daniel Dieterich, ed., *Teaching about Doublespeak* (Urbana, Ill.: National Council of Teachers of English, 1976); William Lambdin, *The Doublespeak Dictionary* (Los Angeles: Pinnacle, 1979); William Lutz, *Doublespeak, from "Revenue Enhancement" to "Terminal Living": How Government, Business, Advertisers and Others Use Language to Deceive You* (New York: Harper and Row, 1981). John Pick, *The Modern Newspeak* (London: Harrap, 1984); William Lutz, ed., *Beyond Nineteen Eighty-Four: Doublespeak in a Post-Orwellian Age* (Urbana, Ill.: National Council of Teachers of English, 1989); and William Lutz, *The New Doublespeak: Why No One Knows What Anyone's Saying Anymore* (New York: HarperCollins, 1996).

60. George Orwell, *1984*, Signet Classic Edition (New York: Penguin, 1950, 1981), 246.

61. Orwell, *1984*, 254.

62. Thus, for example, we can read in David Ogilvy's *Confessions of an Advertising Man* (1963) of "what Madison Avenue calls a 'weasel.'" Whole books indicting "weasel-words" have been compiled by disapproving linguists, who have targeted, especially, "the arty, pseudo-intellectual group, which ranges over the fields of painting, sculpture, music, and literature, particularly of the 'modern' variety," and "the pseudo-scientific array, where physical scientists, psychologists, educators, anthropologists, even linguists, vie with one another." Mario Pei, *Words in Sheep's Clothing* (New York: Hawthorn Books, 1969), 3–4,174.

63. William Shakespeare, *As You Like It*, 2.5.13.

64. "To demonstrate veracity in films, especially in war films, we roll the clock backward and shoot scenes in black and white, which looks more "realistic" than color. The recent discovery of amateur color footage from the late thirties and early forties, showing a tanned and sun-flushed Hitler at a Munich rally in 1939, induces

"a shock of the new" in many viewers. It is the counter-counterintuitive—color film surviving from a time we associate with black-and-white visual culture—that provides the sense of shock." Thomas Doherty, "World War II in Film: What Is the Color of Reality?" *Chronicle of Higher Education*, October 9, 1998, B4.

65. "The Trendy Diet That Sizzles: A Counterintuitive Program Reaches Critical Mass," *Newsweek*, September 6, 1999, 60.

66. Judith Butler, *Gender Trouble* (New York: Routledge, 1990), 136, 138.

67. Barthes, *Criticism and Truth*, 51–52.

68. Elmar Holenstein, *Roman Jakobson's Approach to Language*, trans. Catherine Schelbert and Tarcisius Schelbert (Bloomington: Indiana University Press, 1976), 9.

69. Marianne Moore, *The Complete Poems* (New York: Macmillan, 1967), 36, 266–67.

INDEX